SMALL SPACE GARDENING

THE CAN'T MISS SERIES

Published by Cool Springs Press, a Division of Thomas Nelson, Inc., P.O. Box 141000, Nashville, Tennessee 37214.

First printing 2006
Printed in the United States of America
10 9 8 7 6 5 4 3 2 1

Managing Editor: Mary Morgan
Book Design: Bruce Gore
Production Artist: S.E. Anderson
Cover Photo: Lee Anne White

Cool Springs Press books may be purchased in bulk for educational, business, fundraising, or sales promotional use. For information, please email SpecialMarkets@ThomasNelson.com.

Visit the Thomas Nelson website at **www.ThomasNelson.com** and the Cool Springs Press website at **www.coolspringspress.net.**

photo credits & illustrations

William Adams: 102, 119 (right)

Liz Ball & Rick Ray: 126C, 127A, 129B, 130A, 133C, 134C, 140B, 147BC, 154A, 157A, 158A, 160-161, 162AB

Pam Beck: 149A

Tim Boland and Laura Coit: 159B

Cathy Wilkinson Barash: 7, 45, 51 (top), 53, 98, 116 (bottom), 118 (top)

Barbara Denk: 29 (Garden of George Little and David Lewis), 48 (Garden of Caren and David Anderson), 113 (Garden of Cassie and Doug Picha)

Linda & Alan Detrick: 17, 23, 26-28, 30, 33, 35, 40, 42, 43 (top), 49, 51 (bottom), 55, 57, 59, 68, 100, 103 (top), 107, 109, 110, 111 (top), 116 (top), 117, 120

Tom Eltzroth: 31, 32, 101, 123, 124, 126AB, 127B, 128B, 129AC, 130BC, 131, 132AC, 133AB, 134B, 135-136, 137C, 138A, 139BC, 140AC, 141AC, 142AB, 143AB, 144, 145AB, 146B, 148AC, 149B, 150A, 152AC, 153AC, 154B, 156A, 156C, 157B, 158C, 159AC, 164AB

Lorenzo Gunn: 155B, 163C

Pam Harper: 10, 11, 44, 48, 65, 66, 103(bottom), 112, 113 (right), 115, 118 (bottom), 142C, 147A, 151C, 155A, 156B

Dency Kane: 128A, 153B, 163B, 164C

Peter Loewer: 150B

Robert Lyons: 149C

Dave Mackenzie: 151A

Charles Mann: 150C

Melinda Myers: 8, 43 (bottom), 114, 128C, 132B

Steven Pategas: 151B

Jerry Pavia: 9, 34, 39, 41, 46 (bottom), 47, 99, 104, 105, 106, 108, 111 (bottom), 119 (left), 127C, 137AB, 138BC, 139A, 141B, 143C, 145C, 146AC, 148B, 154C, 155C, 162C, 163A

Felder Rushing: 5, 94, 134A, 152B

Ralph Snodsmith: 158B

Neil Soderstrom: 13, 15, 16, 36, 37, 54, 56, 58, 61, 64 (bottom), 70-78, 83, 86-88, 90-93, 95-97, 121-122

Lee Anne White: 6, 46, 67

David Winger: 64 (top)

Thanks to Mark Thompson of On the Balcony for his assistance with photos.
Design illustrations by Carol Bangs: 18-20, 22
Design diagram conceived by Carol Bangs; production by Bill Kersey: 166

THE CAN'T MISS SERIES

SMALL SPACE GARDENING

MELINDA MYERS

COOL SPRINGS PRESS
A Division of Thomas Nelson Publishers
Since 1798

dedication

To my daughter Nevada who keeps me smiling—you are an amazing young woman. And to all who share their love and friendship—thanks for making my life so rich.

acknowledgements

This was my year to take a break from writing. I was actually going to clean my basement and organize all my slides. Stop laughing—I really was going to get it done this year. But when the opportunity came to share my experiences as a small space gardener, I couldn't resist. Especially when accompanied by an enthusiastic nudge from Cindy Games, Associate Publisher at Cool Springs Press. Her enthusiasm and ability for getting books into the hands of gardeners is contagious. And that goes for publicist Lola Honeybone. Thanks for all your hard work helping me get my message out to gardeners across the country.

And so the process began. As with any endeavor many people helped directly and indirectly to make this book a reality. Mary Morgan was the first to see my words supplemented with photos so I could share my message within this small space. It has been a pleasure and I hope we have a chance to work together again. As Managing Editor Ramona Wilkes took on the challenge of working with me on another project. Thanks for your patience, persistence, and extra effort to make this happen. To Hank McBride and all the other folks at Cool Springs and Thomas Nelson—thanks for the opportunity.

As I worked on the book I felt the combination of words, photos, and illustrations was critical in conveying the message. Thanks to all the photographers who contributed to this book and helped illustrate the beauty and opportunities hidden in a small space. Thanks also to Carol Bangs, Landscape Architect, for her illustrations that will help you put your ideas on paper and eventually into the ground.

The less obvious but very important contributors are those gardeners and professionals that constantly share their knowledge and experience. Thanks to Mark Thompson of On the Balcony for sharing all the new products and furnishings that make small space gardening easier and more exciting. As always, thanks to all the master gardeners, staff at botanical gardens, horticulture educators and professionals who welcome me with open arms sharing their knowledge with me and so many others. Thanks to all the Garden Writers, editors and media professionals who are helping me move my dream forward. The M&M's are on the way! Thanks also to John and Noreen Thiel of Thiel Design for the amazing logo he designed for me (see it on my website www.MelindaMyers.com).

Thanks also to my business team that keeps me on track, moving forward and laughing. Diana Paul you are amazing as you help me grow my business and maintain my sanity. I am grateful to my advisory committee Terry, Jim, Arlene, Dennis, Tisa, Dave, and Heather who so willingly share their time and talents.

And thanks to all the small space gardeners who share their secrets and find creative ways to squeeze one more plant into their gardens.

contents

The Perfect
Small Space

Close your eyes and visualize your ideal small garden. What do you see? Maybe it's a secret hideaway within the larger landscape, or a secluded garden confined to a city lot, or even a lush balcony. Maybe it has a few carefully chosen containers with stunning architectural plants, or it might be crammed with colorful blooms, or it could be a composition of elegant hedges and stonework.

Whether you are trying to create an intimate garden, carve out a cozy outdoor room within your large landscape, or want to try big landscaping ideas in a small space, this book can help. Together, we will go through the process of evaluating your small space as it relates to your and your family's needs. Then we will start building a beautiful garden from the ground up. We will find creative ways to maximize planting space and fill it with plants that have great impact such as year-round interest or added value such as attracting birds and butterflies. We will find creative ways to fill the space with greens and blossoms.

But this book is about more than plants. It is about creating an outdoor living space for you to enjoy looking at and living in. We will discuss furnishings, water and lighting, and other features that make the most of the available space while helping create a beautiful garden.

So whether you are dealing within the confines of a postage-stamp-sized lot, a balcony or small planting space outside your condo, or just trying to create a small garden hideaway or outdoor living space within your larger landscape, this book can help you do it. You can create a wonderful outdoor space no matter your boundaries, schedule, or gardening skill. Now, let's get started on the process that starts with planning and ends with enjoying your outdoor living space.

CAN'T MISS TIP:

EVERYONE CAN PLAY

Get the whole family involved. List all the things you want to do in the garden. Then break out the crayons, paper, glue, scissors, and catalogues. Everyone can draw or create his or her idea of the perfect small space garden. As you compare your pictures and collages, you can look for clues—colors, uses, and other features you may want to include.

1

Getting Started

Analyzing Your Space

So many plants, so little space is the biggest challenge for plant lovers when designing a landscape for their small city lot, balcony, or even their secret garden tucked away within the larger landscape. I have a small city lot and long for the room to grow a mass of something rather than just one of these and one of those.

I have made my whole yard into a garden with just enough grass between the sidewalk and curb to keep the city happy. But there is still not enough room—even with a second story balcony that provides a bit more space to enjoy the outdoors.

Some gardeners solve their space problem by ignoring it. They plant everything they want, cramming it all too close together. This gives instant gratification but lots of headaches and extra work in the long run. More pruning, thinning and pest management are needed to keep these over-planted landscapes functioning in their small area. If you are not careful, some of the plants may be crowded into oblivion by their more aggressive neighbors. This wastes money that could have been spent on permanent plants, a new fence, or that wonderful piece of garden art on your wish list.

Selling your house and buying a bigger lot may be the only real solution to a lack of garden space. But for most of us this is not possible. It may not fit into our budgets or our lifestyles. For me, I like my house and the thought of packing up and moving all my stuff, garden included, is overwhelming. So for now, our solution is creativity!

At the other end of the spectrum, too much space and not enough privacy may be the challenge for those of you with large yards. You long for a retreat from the chaos, privacy from the play areas, a place to meditate, or an intimate outdoor room for entertaining. But the same principles apply when creating the boundaries of your hideaway and filling it with plants and furnishings.

This simple, intimate garden room offers a calming, restful space to sit and chat with friends or read a book.

LOT SURVEY

Now is a good time to pull out your lot survey. You may have it safely stored with your important paper work, or you may need to contact your local municipality for a copy. This survey provides you with useful information about your lot lines, size, and the position of your home on the land. Get a copy of this to help you develop your base map for the landscape design. This is also necessary if you plan to install any fences or permanent structures.

So don't trade in that large lot; let's create a room or two within the larger space. Think of your landscape like a home with multiple rooms. Each has a use and we are about to create your den, reading room or dining area.

Get a Lay of the Land

Make a rough sketch of your balcony or landscape. Don't worry, you don't need to be an artist. Just get out a ruler or other straight edge and a pencil. All you are doing is making straight lines, a few circles, squares and rectangles—nothing fancy. A copy of your lot survey will make this task a bit easier. Eventually we will transfer this drawing to graph paper to make the design process easier. In the meantime, make a copy of your rough sketch or plot plan or use a piece of tracing paper over it to take notes as you tour the area.

Take some measurements as you tour, starting with measuring the outside boundaries. Two sets of hands makes measuring larger spaces easier, but you can do it alone. I use a long-bladed screwdriver or dandelion digger and a long tape measure when working alone. I run the screwdriver through the loop on the end of the tape and anchor it into the ground. It stays in place while I walk out the distance to be measured. You may need to attach a ring or other looping device to the end of your tape. Some gardeners tie the first foot of the tape around the anchor and adjust their measurements

A small urban yard when the design process is just beginning looks like a hopeless project.

accordingly. Be careful not to stretch the tape, which will reduce the accuracy of your measurements.

Or check with friends and neighbors in the landscape or construction business. They may have a measuring wheel to lend you. This tool allows you to measure the distance as you walk. This is not necessary, but it is easier, especially in measuring those curved edges and awkward shapes.

Midway through construction, it's almost impossible to believe this is the same place as in the previous photo, but notice the same buildings beyond the new back wall.

The garden from the previous two photos is now planted, thriving, and gorgeous—the transformation in your garden can be just as dramatic.

Once the outside boundaries are measured, start locating existing plants, planting beds, and structures such as sheds and fences. Measure the distance from the house to the outside boundaries and then to the specific structure or plant to locate it on the plan. Be sure to measure the size of the object so you can include the total space existing items occupy within the landscape.

Note where you currently keep your garbage cans, compost bin and grill. Mark areas where you or your children and pets tend to play, and note high traffic areas and neglected spaces. Look for other items such as bikes, hammocks and lawn furniture that occupy space.

A Room with a View

Take a closer look outside the area where you're making a garden. What views do you want to screen and which do you want to keep? The neighbor's kennel, busy street or noisy play area may include views and sounds you want to eliminate from your garden. Take a chair along with you. First, look at the views as you stand. Then sit and see how they change. Some views may require ground to ceiling screening while others just need screening at seated eye level.

Make note of any existing screening materials. Deciduous plants will lose their leaves in the fall, and you will lose the screening. This is not a problem if you are not using the area during the dormant season after the leaves disappear.

Locate views you want to keep. Borrowed views of a neighbor's beautiful garden, nearby park or city skyline can expand your garden and enhance your enjoyment without adding an inch of planting space. Again, note if and how these desirable views will change throughout the season. You will want to utilize and incorporate the beauty around you whenever possible. It is a cheap and easy way to decorate your space.

Now move indoors. Look into the outdoor garden from various rooms within your house. Note the windows and doors that have a view into the garden you want to enhance. Linking the indoors with the outside can increase the impact of your small garden and make both the indoor and outdoor living areas feel larger.

Consider views you may want to limit or block. A private get-a-way is not so peaceful when your room-mate or children's bedrooms have a direct line of sight into it. You may need to position the furniture or arrange the use of the space to give a view of the garden but not of you.

Linking the indoors with the outside can increase the impact of your small garden.

Now listen to your garden. You may need to screen out noise as much as or more than views. Busy streets, school yards, loud neighbors, and play areas may create more noise than you want to hear. Check the sound levels at different times of the day and on different days of the week. Focus on those times and days you plan to enjoy your garden space. A fence, hedge or multi-layered planting can help soften surrounding noise. Moving water—whether a stream, waterfall, or small fountain—can also do wonders to mask unwanted noise.

Sun and Shade

Locate north and note it on your sketch. This will help you with sun and wind patterns in your garden or on your balcony. Now check out the sun and shade patterns within the yard. Notice how overhangs, trees, hedges, sheds and neighboring homes, structures, and plants impact the sunlight reaching your garden. A south-facing space is not necessarily sunny. Large evergreens, overhangs and a garage could keep this space in shade all day long.

Shade and the object creating the shade may influence the growing conditions for nearby plants. Shaded areas may stay cooler and are less subject to drying winds, resulting in less moisture loss from the plants. On the other hand, shade cast by the dense canopy of trees such as Norway maples not only reduces the amount of light but also of rain water reaching the plants. Plus the competition for water and nutrients from tree roots adds to the stress on plants growing beneath trees.

The sun shining through this Japanese cherry makes beautiful shade patterns underneath—the patterns will change throughout the day and will determine what plants will do well there.

WHAT IS PARTIAL SHADE?

Each gardener and professional has his or her own definition of sun and shade. Then we throw in part sun and part shade to add to the confusion. Some gardeners relate the concept to the weather forecast, saying part sun is a bit sunnier than part shade, just as partially cloudy means there are slightly more clouds than on a partially sunny day.

The University of Nebraska Cooperative Extension further breaks down the definition. Their sketches and definitions are helpful—see their website at http://ianrpubs.unl.edu/horticulture/g1341.htm#types

But I like to keep things simple. So we will look at only a few basic categories and some additional ones that merit definition. As your gardening experience grows, you will fine-tune these definitions to fit your own garden environment and planting experience. And then you will understand why there are so many different definitions floating around.

- **Full sun:** An area that receives eight hours or more of direct sunlight.

- **Part sun:** An area receiving four to six hours of direct sunlight in morning or afternoon.

- **Light shade:** Areas that are bright though shaded much if not all of the day. Some people include dappled or filtered shade in this category. Light shade at mid-day in the peak of summer provides relief from the heat and allows flowers to produce a more brilliant colorful display.

- **Open shade:** These areas are shaded by nearby buildings or fences. There are no overhead trees or structures blocking the sunlight. Just like light shade, these areas may be well lit even though they do not receive direct sunlight.

- **Dappled or filtered shade:** The sun shining through a fine-textured tree canopy or lattice covered arbor creates sun and shade patterns below. As the sun moves across the sky, these patterns change throughout the day. This creates an ever-changing combination of sun and shade.

- **Partial or medium shade:** This occurs in areas shaded for most of the day. They may receive direct sun in the morning or late afternoon. Areas under large shade trees or bright north-facing exposures often fit into this category.

- **Full shade:** These areas have little or no direct sun all day. The only light reaching these areas comes from sunlight reflected off a nearby wall or surface

- **Dense shade:** This can be found under decks and stairways, in heavily wooded areas, and under evergreens branched near the ground. No direct or reflected light reaches these areas.

Visit the balcony or garden at different times of the day to see how the light patterns change. Also consider the changes that occur throughout the year as the sun changes position in the sky and trees gain and lose leaves. The winter sun is lower in the sky, directing more of its light and warmth from the south.

Your location in relation to the equator will also influence light requirements and planting locations. The intense sunlight of the south pushes many sun-loving plants into partially shaded locations. Northern gardeners may need to increase the sunlight to take advantage of additional heat and light from reflected structures and surfaces.

Make note of plants that are thriving or have performed well in the past in various locations. These indicator plants will help you determine what other plants can work well in the area. When helping gardeners assess their landscape and plan for new additions, I ask about the plants that have thrived and failed in the various sites. This gives great insight into the existing light and soil.

This tactic also has helped me make additions in my own yard. My side yard faces south but is shaded by my and my neighbor's two-story houses that are only eight feet apart. One summer I had some leftover salvia and okra that needed a home, and the side yard was the only space available. Both these plants prefer full sun in my Wisconsin landscape, so I did not have great expectations for their performance. To my surprise, both bloomed and to my family's disappointment the ornamental okra produced a bumper crop.

Studying sun and shade patterns is not just for the health of our plants. It is also about including in the design the added benefits of light and shade patterns created by the interaction between plants and sunlight. A backlit plant can glow in the morning or evening as the rising or setting sun provides natural backlighting. I enjoy my silverfeather miscanthus the most in winter. The morning sun shines through the icy seed heads creating a captivating display to view as I sip my morning coffee.

Also note how colors change throughout the day, the season, and with the weather. The light from the mid-day sun can often overpower or wash

The side lighting on this coleus 'Tilt-a-Whirl' makes the purple leaves turn to red.

out the more subtle colors in your landscape. Notice how photographers avoid mid-day shooting and prefer overcast days. The more diffuse sun found early and late or on overcast days creates soft shadows that don't hide the details of the landscape. The more subtle tones and hues of the landscape are also revealed.

Chances are your landscape or at least parts of your landscape will experience all these types of lighting. The angle and direction of sunlight help create a variety of moods, shades of color and visual impact in your small space. Use the notes you make on light, shadow, and color to help you with plant and furniture placement. You want to make sure you create a landscape that provides maximum appeal and that the furniture is situated to enjoy the space at the time you will be there.

As you place your furnishings think about your light preference. Some people prefer to hide in the shade, while others like a bit of sunlight. Recent studies indicate that sunlight improves many aspects of our health and mental attitude. A short, twenty-minute stint in the sun (wearing sunscreen, of course!) can help build bones, reduce sleep disorders, and lower cholesterol. You may get all the sun you need while gardening or playing sports and prefer a shady spot to relax. Or maybe you are trapped in an office all day and want to recharge your solar batteries. Design your space to fit your needs.

Proper pruning of shade trees, use of reflective surfaces, and plant placement help adjust the sunlight to fit your plants' needs and your view. We will discuss ways to deal with shade and increase sunlight in the Chapter 4.

A Gentle Breeze

It is time to use your other senses. Feel the air as it moves through the landscape or across your balcony. Watch flags, laundry and wind chimes as they blow in the breeze. This shows you the direction of the wind. As with light, the wind can change from day to day and throughout the year. Managing the prevailing winds can help expand your plant palette and will influence your plants' health and vigor.

Blocking strong winds can allow you to enjoy a windy location more often. It also prevents damage to tall or tender plants and eliminates damage to containers and accessories that might blow over and break in the wind. Eliminating strong winds allows you to read and do paper work outside or grab a bite to eat without the help of bricks, rocks and other heavy objects holding everything in place. It also eliminates the embarrassing trip to the neighbor's to collect your garden accessories, furnishings and dishes that blew onto their balcony or backyard!

Be careful not to channel all the wind into a narrow opening. Anyone walking down the streets of the Windy City, Chicago, has felt the force of strong winds channeled, in this case by skyscrapers, into a smaller opening. The power is unbelievable and will greatly undermine your enjoyment of the small space.

Well-designed, thoughtfully placed lights not only make walking through the garden easier and safer by night, they make it more beautiful by day.

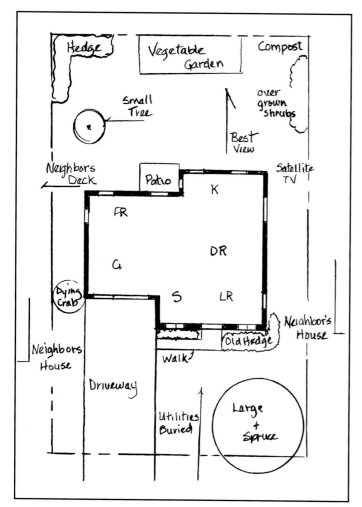

What's on your site now? Sketch the landscape and existing features.

On the other hand, blocking all the wind can eliminate those welcome summer breezes that allow you to tolerate the midsummer heat. Those gentle breezes are also welcome to the plants. Air circulation reduces humidity that is uncomfortable for us and encourages disease problems on our plants.

Diffuse the wind by using lattice fencing, staggered plantings, or intermittent screening. These provide privacy and noise relief as well as reduce the force of the wind. Those unable to tame the occasional strong winds will have to design with that in mind. Balcony dwellers may need to anchor lightweight items to the floor or railings. Many companies are designing outdoor accessories with the wind in mind. Some of us may just need to secure or store items out of the wind when not in use. But proper planning can usually help us tame the wild wind into a gentle breeze to be enjoyed throughout the summer.

Under Your Feet

Now look at the foundation for your small space garden—the soil. A healthy beautiful garden, especially a small one, starts with the soil. Note problem areas where water collects, runs off or erodes the soil. Amending the soil, changing grades, and designing around problem areas can help correct and overcome these obstacles. We will discuss more details and techniques for dealing with these challenges in Chapter 3.

Balcony and patio gardeners get to create their own foundation. Your planting mix will go into a variety of window boxes and pots. The good news is that you determine what goes into the mix. The bad news is that space and weight limitations have a major impact on plant selection, the growing environment, and maintenance. Tips on maximizing the appeal and minimizing the maintenance of container gardens are in Chapter 4.

One Last Look Around

As you consider the ground plane, you need to think about the utilities under your feet. Cable, electric, gas and phone lines may lie beneath. Contact the

DIAL BEFORE DRAWING

Call your utility locating service to make sure you have all underground utilities noted correctly on your base plan. This free service marks all underground utilities such as phone line, gas, cable and electric. Always call before digging in! It could save you money spent repairing the damage your shovel can do and may even save your life. Find the number for your local utility locating service at http://www.digsafe.com/company_one calldirectory.htm or check your phone book or ask your local utility company.

What are the wind, sun and drainage patterns? Put a tracing paper overlay on your original sketch, and note wind, sun and drainage patterns.

utility locating service in your area. They will come to your yard and mark all the underground utilities. Note these on your landscape plan. This free service could save you money and possibly your life. Digging into a fiber optic cable is costly and hitting a gas or electric line is deadly. Give the utility locators a call whenever you are planning landscape renovations or digging in the yard. Allow at least three working days between the time you call and the day you need to start the work.

Look up and note any overhead utilities. Avoid using tall plants below or near overhead wires. Plants growing in utility lines create hazardous situations and maintenance costs in the landscape. Broken branches can down power lines, children can climb trees accessing the power lines, and specially trained arborists will be needed to prune trees growing in or near power lines. Trust me—your utility company does not want to come out and make you remove or severely disfigure your plants to keep them out of the power lines.

Avoid the problem entirely by selecting low-growing trees (less than 25') that won't interfere with overhead wires. These smaller

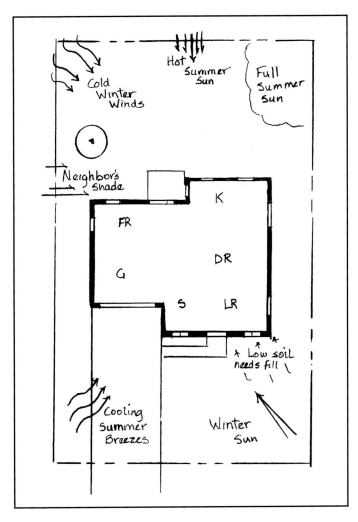

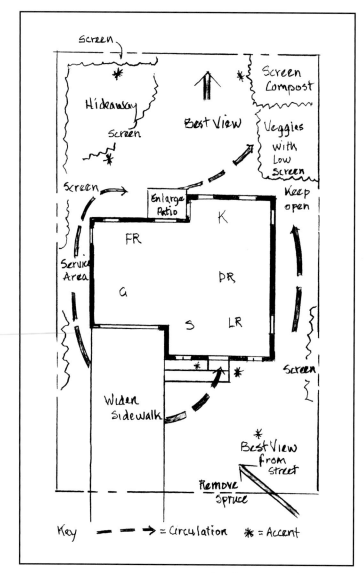

Screen

Hideaway

Screen

Screen

Best View

Screen
Compost

Veggies
with
Low
Screen

Keep
open

Enlarge
Patio

K

FR

Service
Area

DR

G

S

LR

Screen

Widen
Sidewalk

Best View
from
street

Remove
Spruce

Key — — → = Circulation   ✳ = Accent

trees are better suited to small space gardens, in any case. If you do want larger trees, keep those that will reach 25 to 40 feet tall at least 30 feet away, and those over 40 feet tall at least 50 feet away, from utility lines.

Pictures Are Worth 1000 Words

Take pictures of the landscape to help when you move the planning process indoors. Include pictures from inside the house looking out into the space, different perspectives of the space outdoors, and good and bad views from the landscape looking toward your house, neighbors' houses, the street and areas beyond.

Use the camera just as you did the tape measure to help give you a sense of the space within the garden and of the surrounding landscape. You may want to continue this practice throughout the development and installation process. And be sure to take pictures throughout the year. This will help you develop year-round appeal in the garden, identify problems, and record the changes in your landscape as plants grow and the surrounding environment such as buildings, skylines and plants evolves.

Where do you want screening, circulation, and accents? The next layer of your sketch focuses on how to use your space to best advantage.

Putting It All Together

Gather your sketch and all your notes to begin the design process. Graph paper provides a built in measuring grid making it easy to sketch your property, balcony or patio and all its features to scale. Or use plain paper and a ruler or scale to accomplish the same results. This sketch will serve as your base map for future additions.

We're going to start with a sketch of the whole landscape. Those on small properties may use the total landscape to create their perfect small space garden. Those with larger yards will use this to help identify the perfect location for their garden hide-a-way and determine elements it should include. By looking at the whole landscape you will be able to pick the best location for your garden, avoid problems, and maximize benefits. Those restricted to a balcony, patio or one section of the landscape should follow the same process, eliminating unnecessary steps along the way.

The first step is to determine the scale or measuring unit you'll use. This allows you to capture large spaces on paper while keeping them in proportion when reduced in size. Balcony owners may want to use 1 inch to represent every foot of balcony space while those doing an overall design may need to make every inch equal 8 or 10, 16 or 20 feet.

Those using graph paper can also assign a value for each square on the paper. Most graph paper is divided into 4 or 8 squares per linear inch. Use the same scale for all the structures, plants and furnishings included on your design, and record the scale you choose in the corner of the plan for future reference. This is also a good place to indicate which direction is north. Both scale and direction are important in garden planning.

Draw the lot lines or balcony border on the paper. Use the measurements you took or your property survey to determine these figures. Now locate the house, garage or other buildings on the plan. The measurements from the outside borders to the structures will help you properly position these structures within the landscape. Draw these structures to scale.

Include the interior layout of your home to help assess the connection between the indoor and outdoor living space. Mark windows and doors on all structures. This will remind you of views to accent or block, and traffic patterns throughout the landscape and within the small space. Balcony gardeners should include windows and doors that will provide views and access to the balcony garden.

THE MORE, THE MERRIER

Take advantage of everyone's talents and skills when developing your landscape plan. The artist in the family can help with the sketching, the math whiz can take on measurements and spacing, and the gardener can guide the selection of plants. Don't worry if you don't have this team of people to enlist. Ask friends and other family members to lend a hand. It is a great way to renew friendships and learn from each other. If you still can't find any willing participants, then enjoy the fact that doing all the work yourself entitles you to make all the decisions.

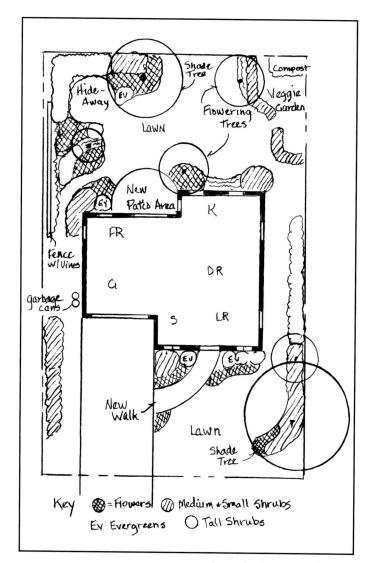

Key ⊕ = Flowers ⦸ Medium + Small Shrubs
     Ev Evergreens ◯ Tall Shrubs

As the last step before a real design, do a sketch that captures your overall concept with general placement of walks, patios, and plants. This is the final layer before you start drawing your plan.

Include walks, decks, patios, permanent beds and plants you will preserve. Don't include items you plan to eliminate. Draw overhead and underground utilities, septic tank leach beds and septic tanks that need to be considered when selecting the area for and designing your small space garden.

This drawing is your base map that will be preserved throughout the planning process. Use layers of tracing paper to record other information collected in your landscape assessment and for planning purposes. These layers will rest over the base map, allowing you to explore different design possibilities while preserving the base map.

Balcony gardeners should not skip this step. Include posts, support structures, light fixtures, or other permanent features that may impact plant and furniture placement. Note railing height and other permanent aspects of the space.

The next step is to capture all the observations you made related to the environment within your landscape. This is your lot analysis. Note sun and shade patterns, wind direction, low spots and slopes. Indicate traffic patterns worn into the lawn or planting beds. If space allows, include information on the area around your yard. Note good and bad views into the neighboring areas and the landscape beyond. Record the areas where wind and noise barriers are needed.

Time for Input

Gather family members, friends and partners who will be using the balcony, landscape or small space garden. Take a few minutes to go over the survey in this chapter. Some of the information you gathered when developing your base map and site analysis. You may want to review these items with others so everyone has the same core information to work from. They may also help you uncover items missed on your survey.

Now start looking at how the landscape is used. Those with large lots may be able to take all the service features such as compost bins, garbage cans, fruit and vegetable gardens and play areas out of the small space.

Those with a balcony or small lot may need to include these in their small space garden.

Place another piece of tracing paper over the base map and site analysis. Identify areas of use for the different parts of the landscape. Those with large lots can treat their landscape like a home with separate rooms. Each room in the landscape can meet a certain need such as storage, entertaining or food gardening. Those with balconies or small lots may need to deal with their space as one does an efficiency or studio apartment—mixing all the necessary uses into one large area.

Careful planning and space-efficient planting techniques can help maximize limited planting space. Many flowering plants are colorful, edible or good for cutting. Many of these same plants are fragrant and attract butterflies and birds. Currants, dwarf apple trees, and strawberries can all be used in place of traditional shrubs, trees and groundcovers. See Chapters 2 and 4 for more specifics on including specialty gardens on your balcony or in a small space.

The serenity and simplicity of a Japanese-style garden have enduring appeal but these gardens can be difficult to design well.

What's Your Style?

Now that you have an idea of available space, its potential uses, and the needs of all involved, it is time to do some visualization. Close your eyes and picture a beautiful garden. Maybe it contains your favorite flowers from childhood, a butterfly flitting through the air, and colorful fragrant blooms to delight all your senses. Remember this image and use it to help guide you through the design process.

Are the plants in your imagined garden neatly arranged in rows in front of sheared hedges or are they casually grouped as large masses in curved beds winding throughout the yard? Are there lots of straight lines and man-made structures, or do curves and natural materials predominate? The answers to these questions will help you determine a style for your landscape.

CAN'T MISS TIP:

COMPUTER HELP

Computer-aided landscape design programs are available online and at garden centers, book stores, and other locations selling software. Some can be very useful in helping you lay out the existing landscape and guiding you through the process of adding new features and plants to the yard. For some, the technology is great motivation, while for others it interferes with the process or distracts from the goal of designing a new landscape.

LANDSCAPE DESIGN SURVEY

Use this or a similar tool to help you gather information from and share it with those significant people in your life who will be using the small space garden or balcony. These questions will help you capture your thoughts and organize the information needed to design your small space garden.

Site Information

Share the base map you developed with others involved. Review your observations and ask for their observation and feedback on the following:

• Existing features

The color and architecture of the house _____

_____

Color and architecture or style of other structures

Garage _____

_____

_____

Shed _____

_____

Other _____

_____

_____

The style and materials of the balcony, deck or patio to be landscaped _____

_____

• Walks

Materials and pattern _____

_____

• Utilities

Overhead

Underground

• The environment

Sun and shade patterns _____

_____

Areas where you need to create shade_____

_____

_____

• Wind direction

Summer _____ Winter _____

Areas where wind screens are needed? _____

_____

_____

Areas where sound buffers are needed _____

_____

_____

• Soil (addressed in Chapter 3)

Type

Amendments needed

Berms, raised beds or other planting strategies

employed

• Drainage concerns

Downspout and sump pump outlet

Soggy areas

Drainage patterns throughout the area

• Slopes

Planting for erosion control needed

Retaining walls needed

• Existing trees, shrubs and planting beds

Identify those to keep and those to eliminate

• Other features such as pool, satellite dish, hot tub . . .

_____

_____

_____

• Views to keep _____

_____

_____

• Views to eliminate _____

_____

_____

Family Wants and Landscape Needs

• Who will use the small space (adults, children, pets)
• How will it be used
  • Entertaining
    How many people
  • Family dining
  • Quiet reflection and reading
  • Meditation and yoga
  • Storage of furniture, tools . . .
  • Composting
  • Water garden
  • Fruit, vegetables and herbs
  • Cut flowers
  • Attracting birds and butterflies
• When will the space be used and for what type of activities: (you may be able to double your use if different people use the space at different times for various purposes)
    Time of day
    Days of the week

Months of the year
- Prioritize the way you will use the space

Landscape Style

- Formal
    Symmetrical
    Straight line beds
    Green as the predominant color
    Minimal diversity in plantings
    Other elements
- Informal
    Asymmetrical
    Curving lines
    Color theme
    Diversified plantings
    Other elements
- Naturalistic
    Informal plus mimics nature
- Natural
    Native plants
    Mimic plant communities of the region
- Stylistic
    Japanese
    Chinese
    Other
- Additional features
    Outdoor lighting for
        Extend use of your small space
        Beauty
        Security
- Landscape Maintenance
    Level preferred
        Low
        Medium
        High
- Water supply
- Ground layer to weed/maintain
    Grass
    Groundcover
    Mulch
    Hard surfaces

- Pruning needs
    Deadheading flowers
    Shearing
    Espalier
    Maintain natural form
- Plant consideration
    Types of plants you like
        Annuals, perennials, flowering shrubs, evergreens , , ,
    Will you include a lawn area
        Is there access for the mower
    Additional features
    Fragrance
    Favorite colors _____
    _____
    _____
    _____

    Least favorite colors _____
    _____
    _____
    _____

    Plant, bee or other allergies to consider
    Deer, rabbits or other wildlife concerns
    Special gardens to include
        Roses, herbs, food, cutting
- Other_____
_____
_____
_____
_____
_____
_____
_____
_____
_____
_____
_____
_____
_____
_____
_____
_____
_____

Now see how your vision fits with your home's architecture, the rest of your landscape, and the neighborhood. The landscape style and elements within the yard should complement your home. My home is a brick Tudor, and my front yard is a garden. I use brick pavers at my entrance and steppers through the garden made of a local stone called lannon. This provides a link between the landscape and the more formal look and elements of my home.

Your landscape doesn't have to conform to neighborhood design styles, but you may want it to feel like it belongs in the block rather than looking out of place. This is why I kept some grass and used pavers in my small front garden. They provide a sense of order and continuity with the neighboring homes while maintaining my informal garden style.

Formal versus Informal

Pull all your thoughts and visions together and get to work on developing a landscape style. The two major types are formal and informal. Many of the small space gardens of the past were formal in appearance. The tidy garden beds were geometrically shaped and filled with rows of annuals that fronted neatly trimmed hedges or brick walls. The plantings were symmetrical, providing a sense of balance and unity through repetition of plants, form and color.

These gardens usually contained formal statuary, cement fountains and classically designed urns filled with flowers and vines. One of these features often served as a focal point that the garden was designed around. The straight lines of the plantings and beds make the eyes move quickly through the landscape. The neat, organized beds provided a sense of orderliness and control over nature.

If the ideal garden you visualized included knot gardens, topiaries and beds filled with meticulously groomed plants, you should consider a formal design. Look for plants that tolerate shearing and structures that are classic in shape and materials.

The breezy informality of a cottage garden is quite deceptive—this relaxed style of garden still needs maintenance to keep it from becoming a mess.

If your imagined garden was of a cottage garden with curved lines, masses of plants and free flowing curves, an informal design probably is more your style. Informal gardens create balance through a mixture of plants that repeat form and texture. They are asymmetrical with curved lines, intermingling plants and more natural materials.

You can take the informal style one step further and look to nature for inspiration. A naturalistic landscape is designed to mimic those elements found in nature. Less control is exerted over the plants, giving the more casual style you would expect to see in a natural area.

If you want a natural garden design, substitute native plants for traditional garden favorites, and plant them in arrangements similar to your region's native plant communities. Nature provides many examples of small space gardens within its larger plant communities. Take a hike to a few natural areas to gather ideas to incorporate in your small space design.

Minimalism is a low maintenance approach to the formal garden. The ground layer is mulch or a paved surface that doesn't require mowing and needs only minimal weed control. Sheared hedges are replaced with brick walls or low maintenance fencing materials. The goal is to create a pleasant formal garden requiring little effort.

Or maybe you want your small space to reflect a certain garden style. We think of French gardens as filled with geometric beds surrounded by short clipped hedges. These beds may contain grass, herbs, vegetables or flowers. The plantings within the beds change throughout the year and over time. Small space gardens have often been based on Renaissance gardens with their enclosed courtyards. Add some water, a forest of columns, citrus plants and a geometric arrangement to capture the elements of a Spanish landscape. Japanese landscape design incorporates religious and philosophical symbolism into a naturalistic style. Chinese gardens are known for their meticulous and decorative informality and continuity. Carefully selected plants and stones, bridges, and pools are just a few of the elements found in these gardens. These are just a few stylistic garden approaches you may want to consider.

This formal Charleston-style garden has traditional boxwood hedges, classical statuary, and lovely, mossy brick paving— proving that beauty can lie in structure, not colorful blooms.

All the Pieces Make a Whole Design

No matter the style, your design will incorporate the same basics. The lines of the beds, walkways and plantings will influence the look and feel of the overall landscape. Straight lines make the eye travel quickly through the space. Jagged and vertical lines create a sense of excitement, while gentle curves and horizontal lines slow down the eye creating a restful feel.

Form is the shape created by the lines in the garden. The plants, beds and accessories are the forms our eyes notice as we look into a garden. Consider the landscape forms that stand out in your memory. They may include a spiral topiary juniper, weeping katsura tree, columnar ginkgo or spreading crabapple. These forms can be repeated to create a sense of unity throughout the garden, or each can be used singly as a focal point.

The exciting and challenging aspects of garden design are the ever-changing elements we work with. Plants grow and change throughout the seasons, during the year and over time. These changes in form over time add interest to the garden's design. Permanent features such as walls, structures and edgers are more constant, providing continuity within the changing scene.

Plants, and to some extent structural features, provide texture, fragrance and color in the garden. These can be used to achieve balance and unity, or they can also be used to create a focal point or area of emphasis within the garden. Chapter 2 discusses design principles more fully.

The difference between a colorful plant collection and a designed garden are the unifying features that pull it all together. Repetition of lines, forms, textures, colors or individual plants help unify the landscape. This cohesiveness can stave off the sense of chaos that often makes a small garden appear even smaller.

But don't forget to include a bit of variety. This is what grabs

The stone of the house is echoed in the stone of the path and stairway, while the lush, informal plantings soften the stonework, creating a harmonious whole of the house and its setting.

FOR THE BALCONY

The straight lines, metal and steel materials and rectangular shape of the balcony give it a formal look and sometimes a cold unwelcoming feel. Soften these features and warm up the space with planters. A small grouping of containers arranged in front of the corner post or a pot filled with a feathery ornamental grass can mask the harsh angle with a gentle curve.

Use trailing plants to cover the railings, posts and other structural elements of the balcony. A sweet potato vine or licorice plant will quickly fill a pot and cascade over the hanging basket or railing planter.

Use a uniquely shaped plant, a piece of garden art, or another colorful item to create a focal point on the balcony. This can lead the eye to an area you want to highlight and away from the neighbor's balcony, air conditioning unit, or other less desirable view.

your attention and holds your interest. A unique plant combination, unusual plant form or rarely seen specimen can create a focal point without disrupting the overall flow of the garden.

Within the garden and the overall landscape there should be a sense of balance, with all parts of the garden equally weighted. In the formal garden, each half or quadrant of the garden mirrors the other. The informal garden is also balanced but in an asymmetrical manner. The attention commanded by each half of the garden is equal because each side, though not identical, is balanced in terms of points of interest.

Consider scale when designing the space and selecting plants. Plants that are in proportion to the house and neighboring plants look as though they belong and are part of the overall community. Initially the garden may be out of proportion due to the small size of immature plants. Some gardeners include structures and other features to provide scale until the plants grow into their mature size and fit with the house, the remainder of the garden and any nearby buildings.

Design Tricks for Small Spaces

Keep all the design elements and principles in mind when designing your small

This colorful, exuberant garden creates just the right setting for a creatively painted bungalow—both house and garden shout "look at me!"

The diamond-shaped window in the trellis at the end of this patio provides both a view outside and a place to showcase a bright hanging basket.

space. You may also need to employ a few tricks to help make it appear larger.

Selecting dwarf plants will give the look of larger specimens without gobbling up limited room. The shorter size of a dwarf plant will be more in scale to the small garden but the plant's form will be reminiscent of its larger relatives. Keep in mind that dwarf simply means smaller than the standard species; it doesn't necessarily mean small. So check the label before purchasing any plant to make sure it will still fit the space you have for it when it reaches mature size.

Place small plants next to tall ones. A drastic height change causes the eye to quickly rise from ground level, creating the illusion of greater depth in the bed and more space in the garden.

Cut out windows in walls and fencing or leave openings in hedges to allow for borrowed views. Opening up the garden to the beauty that surrounds your small space allows you to take advantage of someone else's hard work while extending the boundaries of your small hide-away.

Some gardeners have incorporated mirrors into their landscapes. Hung on a wall behind a statue or strategically placed to reflect the garden, mirrors can create the illusion the garden goes well beyond its limited boundaries. Interior designers have been using this technique for years.

Keep larger-leafed plants near the front of the garden, and back them with smaller foliaged plants. This contrast in size—with smaller leaves appearing to be in the distance—helps make the backdrop appear farther away than it is. This creates the illusion of greater depth in the bed and more space in the garden.

Use pavers that echo the brick on the house or the flooring on the adjoining indoor room. This ties the house, garden and indoor space together creating the feel of a great room, but in this case, half of the great room is outdoors.

Use simple patterns and small pavers to avoid overwhelming the garden with the hard surface. Large steppers and busy patterns can make a small space feel even smaller. Simplicity is the key to creating a beautiful small space garden. Less does not have to be less impressive. Just make sure each element counts. There are more ideas on this in the next chapter.

Adjust the Thermostat

Use design techniques and planting strategies to create a more comfortable outdoor space. Adding a vine-covered arbor or small shade tree can cool off a

COOL GROUND

Groundcover and turf have a cooling effect from evapotranspiration (the loss of water from the soil by evaporation and by the transpiration of the plants growing therein). The temperature above a groundcover will be 10 to 15 degrees cooler than the temperature above a heat-absorbent material such as asphalt or a reflective material such as light-colored gravel or rock.

A heat-absorbent material such as asphalt will also continue to radiate heat after the sun has set. It is best to either minimize the use of heat-absorbent and reflective materials near a house or shade them from any direct sun.

space by as much as 10 degrees. It can also reduce cooling and heating costs indoors if located next to the house and over the air conditioner.

Use arbors with open weave or slatted coverings. An arbor covered with 1- to 2-inch slats of long-lasting wood spaced at least several inches apart will provide plenty of shade while allowing the humidity to escape and cool breezes to blow through. A more open arbor can be used if plants will cover the structure and provide additional shade. Northern gardeners may prefer this strategy, since a deciduous vine on an open arbor allows more warming sunlight through during the cooler weather from fall through spring.

Covering the soil with plants such as groundcover or grass also can help keep the garden space cool. The temperatures above groundcovers can be 10 to 15 degrees cooler than those above a heat-absorbing material such as light-colored gravel or rock. This makes a big difference in your outdoor living space and can also reduce cooling needs inside.

Northern gardeners wanting to extend their outdoor enjoyment may want to use deciduous plants. These allow sunlight into the space during the cool days of spring and summer while shading the areas from hot summer sun. Use paved surfaces under shade-producing features. The pavers will absorb heat in spring and summer and radiate it into the space for added warmth. The summer shade will minimize the absorption and radiation of heat by pavers.

Design with Maintenance in Mind

No matter what garden style you choose, even minimalist, some level of maintenance will be required. Landscape architect Gary Smith said it well, "A garden is the expression of your relationship with the earth. How many relationships have you ever been in that haven't required some form of caring? Relationships aren't maintenance free and neither are gardens."

A lot of work goes into maintaining a beautiful formal garden. Just keeping the grass neatly trimmed around all the corners and edges in this garden is a time-consuming job.

This pleasant side garden is quite easy to maintain—notice how the grass can be cut along the curving edge of the brick path by simply running the mower wheels on the edge of path, so no hand-trimming is required.

An informal garden filled with carefully selected plants can require less maintenance.

Fortunately, with a small space garden there is less to maintain. But you may have chosen a small garden because you do not have the time to manage a large landscape. So as you plan your space, keep maintenance in mind. The design style, plants, structures and paving materials used all influence the amount of maintenance you will need to provide. But some maintenance is not a bad thing. Tending the garden may become your meditation time, weeding may be the way you view your plants, and pruning can be a great workout eliminating a trip to the gym. It is all in the way you look at it.

Formal landscapes tend to require the most maintenance. Keeping plants neatly shaped or trained as topiaries or espaliered into a fence means more pruning. The more you prune, the more brush there is to manage, and that is extra work. An informal garden filled with carefully selected plants can require less maintenance. If you select plants that naturally grow the size and shape you want, minimal pruning will be needed to keep them within the available space.

Use a diversity of plants. This can be difficult in a small space where we are aiming for more simplistic designs to provide the illusion of more room. But mixing up the planting a bit reduces the risk of insects and disease decimating the garden. If a pest problem does occur you will only have a few plants, not the whole hedge, to manage.

Curved beds free of hard to reach corners and angles are generally easier to maintain. The line doesn't have to be perfect, and the mower can easily be guided around the edge. If a lawn is included in your small space, make sure you can reach it with the mower. Small patches of grass can be harder to manage than an extensive lawn if it is difficult to get the mower into the area and move it around. A groundcover or paved surface may be a better alternative.

Access to water is critical for the establishment and maintenance of your garden. Even drought-tolerant plants and xeriscapes need water to get the plants' roots established and keep the young plants growing. Containers, often a big part of small space gardens, need attention on a daily basis.

Place the garden within reach of the water source. Consider time- and water-saving strategies such as soaker hoses incorporated into the planting beds, timers, and other devices that allow you to place the water where and when it is needed.

Group plants with similar water requirements together. Use organic mulches such as woodchips, shredded leaves, or pine straw on the soil surface to conserve moisture and save time spent watering and weeding.

Design space for your tools. If they are handy, you are more likely to use them when needed. And tending the garden for short periods throughout the season is often less stressful than the marathon catch-up work day so many of us find ourselves doing.

These water-loving plants are grouped together, making them healthier and easier to maintain, since they all enjoy the same conditions.

When You're Done

Now that you have your landscape space drawn to scale on paper, you've made a list of potential uses for the space, and you have a landscape style in mind, it is time to design your new garden. We hope you discovered a little more planting space than you originally thought was available, gathered some creative ideas, or maybe just narrowed your expectations of what you want to accomplish in your small space. In any case, you have the basis for designing a beautiful small space garden.

Don't let the next steps of selecting the plants, features and accessories scare you. Think of it like decorating your home. And fortunately our most common garden decorations—plants—are often beautiful enough to hold their own in a less than ideal landscape design. If a plant winds up being in the wrong place, moving it is an easy solution.

We all have the ability to create an attractive garden. For some it comes easy, while for others it is a matter of trial and error. But if you start with a plan, select plants suited to their location, and consider color, texture, and size, you really can't miss.

2

The Fun Begins

Designing Your Garden

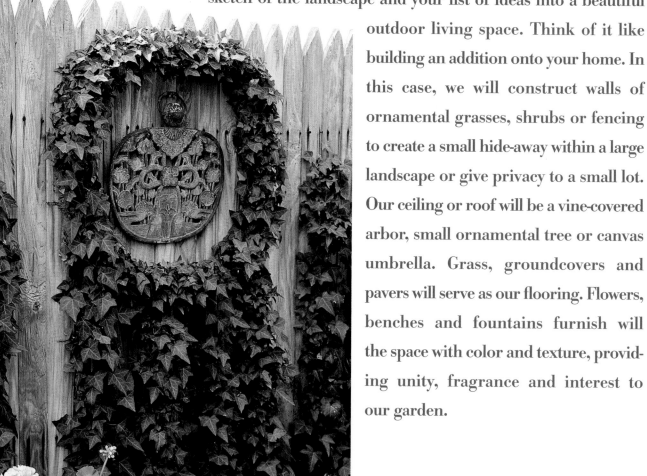

t he exciting part of turning your small space into a garden is about to begin. You are going to transform your sketch of the landscape and your list of ideas into a beautiful outdoor living space. Think of it like building an addition onto your home. In this case, we will construct walls of ornamental grasses, shrubs or fencing to create a small hide-away within a large landscape or give privacy to a small lot. Our ceiling or roof will be a vine-covered arbor, small ornamental tree or canvas umbrella. Grass, groundcovers and pavers will serve as our flooring. Flowers, benches and fountains furnish will the space with color and texture, providing unity, fragrance and interest to our garden.

Cover It Up

Let's start from the top down. The canopy we choose for our small space will influence the types of plants we can use below. An open air garden letting in maximum sun allows us to use some sun-loving plants down below. A vine-covered structure or the branches of a tree provides us with shade throughout the hot summer but may also limit our choice of plants to fill the garden.

You may want to create a combination of sun and shade within your small space. An arbor covering the sitting area, a strategically placed small tree, or an umbrella-clad table may provide you with shelter from the sun while letting in the light for sun-loving shrubs and flowers. Or your small space garden may be situated in the shelter of a large shade tree from your own or your neighbor's yard eliminating the need to create a ceiling.

A charming arbor provides the ceiling over a table and chairs creating a pleasant outdoor dining room.

Pull out your sketch of the garden and look at how the small space will be used. Where do you want shade to relax in and where do you want to let the sun shine through? Perhaps you like to sit in the morning sun as you sip coffee before charging off to work. Or maybe you seek mid-day shade so you can sit and read a good book on a hot summer afternoon.

One family I know created a cozy dining area within their small space garden. A grapevine-clad wooden arbor covered the patio. As the summer temperatures rose, the grape leaves expanded, casting cooling shade. By fall, the clusters of grapes hung down through the arbor's support to add colorful atmosphere to the outdoor dining space.

You may want to grow your own edible canopy of grapes, kiwi, cucumber or squash. Or maybe you prefer an ornamental awning of bird's nest gourds, American bittersweet or bougainvillea or something fragrant like sweet autumn clematis or jasmine. Select the canopy that will work best for you and position it to provide the shelter you desire, keeping in mind the changes your ceiling will undergo during the season.

The tree canopy substitutes for an umbrella sheltering this rustic patio—notice how the style of the furniture and of the garden complements the house.

Northern gardeners may want to use deciduous plants for their ceilings. In spring and fall the leafless plants will let in more of the sun's warmth, extending the use of this space. Southern gardeners may want to create the maximum shade to provide relief from the sun's hot rays for themselves and their plants.

Trace some of the templates from page 166 for small trees, arbors or umbrellas, and start positioning them on your sketch. This may help you get a feel for how to position your ceiling. And keep in mind the ceiling will need to be anchored to the ground. A small tree will need a plot of well-drained soil, an arbor requires a building to anchor to or ground to sink footings in, and an umbrella must have a flat surface for its base to rest upon.

Whatever ceiling you choose, make sure it fits with your overall design. A contemporary trellis or brightly colored umbrella can steal the show and ruin the look of a cottage garden. Select structures made of materials that complement your design. Include plants that provide seasonal interest without dropping lots of debris on you and the surface below. Avoid pest-prone plants that require more maintenance and invite unwelcome visitors to the garden.

Make sure the tree, arbor or furniture is incorporated into the overall design. An arbor sitting in the middle of the lawn, leading to and from nowhere, looks out of place. Set it next to a building and surround it with plants, or place it at the entrance to the garden, and it has a purpose and belongs in that place. The same goes with plants. A lone tree can be dramatic, but it can also look like an afterthought. There is little room for lone stars in a small space garden. Instead set that ornamental tree in a planting bed with a bench beneath, or position it in front of a building or structure to maximize its impact.

CONSIDER PESTS

When selecting plants for a sitting area, avoid those that are highly attractive to bees and wasps if you have family members who are nervous about or sensitive to stings.

Walls and Dividers

As we move toward the ground layer, we need to consider the exterior walls of our hide-away as well as the interior dividers within the space. A good fence not only makes for better neighbors, it also can create the walls that define our small garden within a large yard or provide privacy from nearby neighbors and passers-by if a small garden or balcony is the whole landscape. But a solid fence or dense hedge may make you, as it does me, a bit claustrophobic and can make your already small space feel even smaller. It can also be a bit boring—like a room with white walls and no paintings for visual relief.

Fortunately you can create a sense of space, gain some privacy and still have a beautiful garden to enjoy. Refer back to your landscape sketch, revisiting the views you felt needed blocking and those you wanted to keep. Review the plan, and make sure you have accounted for all the views— both those looking out from within the garden and those from outside into the garden.

Creating an open air space that is private is not as hard as it may seem. I have a second story balcony off the back of my home. The north side overlooks a grassy lot filled with trees. In fact, sitting on my balcony looking out makes me feel like I am in the tree tops. The view to the east overlooks my back garden and into the alley. I enjoy the second-story view of my flowers, but I'm not always thrilled with seeing the alley and the activity there. The view to the south is straight into the second floor of my neighbor's house. The key to making the most of my balcony was maintaining the good views and softening the less desirable ones.

Ornamental grasses screen a seating area from the rest of the garden, while the umbrella provides a ceiling.

A VARIETY OF VINES

For sun:

- **American bittersweet** (*Celastrus scandens*) zones 3–8 (full sun)
- **'Arctic Beauty' kiwi** (*Actinidia kolomikta* 'Arctic Beauty') zones 4–8 (sun to part shade)
- **Black-eyed Susan vine** (*Thunbergia alata*) annual hardy zones 10–11 (sun to part shade)
- **Boston ivy** (*Parthenocissus tricuspidata*) zones 4–8 (sun to shade)
- **Bougainvillea** (*Bougainvillea*) tropical wintered indoors, hardy zones 9–11 (full sun)
- **Canary vine** (*Tropaeolum peregrinum*) used as annual, hardy zones 9–10 (full sun)
- **Cardinal vine** (*Ipomoea* x *sloteri* or *I. coccinea*) annual (full sun to light shade)
- **Clematis** (*Clematis*) zones 3–9 (full sun)
- **Climbing rose** (*Rosa* species) zones 2–8 (full sun)
- **Cypress vine** (*Ipomoea quamoclit*) annual (full sun to light shade)
- **Dutchman's pipe** (*Aristolochia*) zones 5–9 (full to part sun)
- **English ivy** (*Hedera helix*) zones 4–9 (sun to shade) invasive in some areas
- **Euonymus** or **Bigleaf wintercreeper** (*Euonymus fortunei* 'Vegetus') zones (4)5–9 (sun to shade)
- **Five leaf akebia** (*Akebia quinata*) zones 4–8 (sun [can be aggressive] to shade)
- **Grape** (*Vitis*) zones 4–9 (full sun for best fruit)
- **Hops** (*Humulus*) zones 4–8 (full sun to part shade)

- **Hyacinth bean** (*Lablab pupureus*) (*Dolichos lablab*) annual, hardy in zones 10–11 (full sun)
- **Jasmine** (*Jasminum*) zones 6–10 (full to part sun)
- **Firecracker vine** (*Ipomoea lobata* formerly *Mina lobata*) annual (full sun to part shade)
- **Mandevilla** (*Mandevilla*) annual, hardy in zones 10–11 (full to part sun)
- **Morning glory** (*Ipomoea pupurea* or *I. tricolor*) annual, hardy zones 10–11—invasive in some areas (full sun to light shade)
- **Passion flower** (*Passiflora*) zones 6–10 (full to light shade)
- **Porcelain berry vine** (*Ampelopsis brevipedunculata*) zones 4–8—invasive in some areas (full sun to part shade)
- **Scarlet runner bean** (*Phaseolus coccineus*) annual, hardy zones 10–11 (full sun)
- **Sweet pea** (*Lathyrus odoratus*) annual that reseeds and can become weed (full to part sun)
- **Sweet potato vine** (*Ipomoea batatas* cultivars) annual, hardy zones 9–11—trailer that can be trained up support (full to part sun)
- **Trumpet honeysuckle** (*Lonicera*) zones 4–9 (sun to shade)
- **Trumpet vine** (*Campsis radicans*) zones 4–9 (full sun)
- **Virginia creeper** (*Parthenocissus tricuspidata*) zones 3–8—aggressive (sun to shade)
- **Wisteria** (*Wisteria*) zones 5–9 (full sun)

For shade:

- **Boston ivy** (*Parthenocissus tricuspidata*) zones 4–8 (sun to shade)
- **Climbing hydrangea** (*Hydrangea petiolaris*) zones 4–9 (part to full shade)
- **English ivy** (*Hedera helix*) zones 4–9 (sun to shade) invasive in some areas
- **Euonymus** or **Bigleaf wintercreeper** (*Euonymus fortunei* 'Vegetus') zones (4)5–9 (sun to shade)

- **Five leaf akebia** (*Akebia quinata*) zones 4–8 (sun [where it can be aggressive] to shade)
- **Trumpet honeysuckle** (*Lonicera*) zones 4–9 (sun to shade)
- **Virginia creeper** (*Parthenocissus tricuspidata*) zones 3–8—aggressive (sun to shade)

I chose to leave the treescape in full view—that part was easy. A hanging basket filled with blue-flowered plants brightened up the green without diminishing the view. It also added visual balance to the overall décor. I added some larger hanging baskets of trailing strawberries, lavender, ivy geranium, and purple and pink million bells at the southeast corner to screen out much of the alley while framing the view of my garden. Then I added a large palm to provide privacy for my neighbor and myself by blocking the view from the inside out and from the outside in on the south side of the balcony. This along with careful positioning of the furniture and the addition of a fragrant jasmine made my balcony a very enjoyable place to be.

This perfectly placed arbor leads from the flower garden to a small lawn and also provides a home for a luxuriant climbing rose.

Screening Ideas

Combinations of small trees, shrubs, grasses and other plants can provide screening where needed. One savvy business-owner screened the view of the

CREATING THE ILLUSION OF SPACE

Make your small space garden or balcony appear bigger than it actually is.

- **Use cool colors of blue, green and violet.** They tend to recede giving the illusion of space.
- **Minimize the clutter.** Fewer planters, less artwork and a limited amount of furnishings will make your small area feel more spacious.
- **Link your outdoor living space with the indoors.** Repeat tile patterns, building materials, colors and themes for a unified feel that ties the two separate spaces together creating a sense of a much larger space.

parking lot using small trees underplanted with short shrubs and groundcover. The spaces between the different layers of plants gave a sense of openness, while the plants blocked the less than desirable view. You could do the same with plants, planters, or a combination of the two.

Lattice screening hides pool filtering equipment from view and also is a perfect backdrop for trellised shrubs and showy tulips.

One handy gardener—certainly not me!—created her own living screen. She built a frame and filled it with a combination of planters and hooks for hanging baskets. The colorful plants gave a sense of privacy while still allowing the owner to see into the rest of the yard when the children were playing. Or you could try a combination of plants and screening. Two pieces of lattice joined at the corner screen the view from two perspectives. A large planter filled with tall colorful plants adds another layer of screening and improves the view.

The less handy gardeners among us can buy planters with built in privacy trellises. They are perfect for patios, balconies and other areas where

CREATIVE PLANT SUPPORTS

I love to go on garden tours in my community, my state and the whole country. I get so many good ideas and great inspiration on these visits. Here are a few clever ideas I found that you might enjoy.

- **A garden bench no longer safe for sitting** provided the perfect support for a crawling plant.

- **A set of old long handled tools** tied together like a teepee supported a planting of beans. The wooden handles were anchored into the ground and the hoe, rake or cultivator head was clearly displayed on top. It was cute but a little scary at the same time.

- **Old sections of fencing** can add charm, a sense of history, and some needed support.

- **A child's play structure** long outgrown can be left in place but neatly tucked away under cover of an attractive vine.

- **Living and dead trees** can provide the perfect support. Do not use twining vines on living trees. They can girdle and eventually kill the tree. Make sure standing dead trees are not a hazard. A vine-covered tree on your house wouldn't be a pretty sight.

planting space is limited but privacy is desired. A large planter backed by a lattice screen or a decorative metal trellis can set off the planting while blocking the view beyond. Saddle planters that straddle railings and window boxes mounted on the railings can lend a bit of colorful privacy to your balcony or deck if you combine tall and trailing plants in them. These planters come in a variety of styles, colors and lightweight materials. Faux terra cotta, fiberglass with a metallic veneer, and decorative iron frames for fiber liners are just a few of the options. Match the planter style, color and material to your overall landscape design.

And as more gardeners move to smaller spaces, more materials are available. No longer is lattice your only choice for screening. Bamboo, canvas and other decorative outdoor screens are now available. Use the material that best fits the landscape design and mood you are trying to create. Use a bamboo screen as a divider for a tropical or Japanese garden, and a wattle fence for an informal or cottage garden. Check your favorite garden center, outdoor living center, catalogues or web sites for more ideas.

Fences and Walls

Fences can provide a combination of screening and security. You may have inherited a chain link fence with your property, or you may be considering a fence for one or all of the walls of your garden. Take some time to explore all the options.

Lattice fencing can provide an open screen and be an attractive backdrop for plants while adding a bit of charm to a country or contemporary garden. A solid fence with a lattice border on top provides more privacy while retaining a soft edge and a bit of an open feel. Ornamental iron fences are more expensive but can provide security while maintaining the view with a touch of elegance and Victorian charm. Newer fence designs are more contemporary and complement a wider array of landscape styles.

One benefit of small space gardens is you need fewer materials. I live in the city and have a small lot. Surrounding my back yard with a 6-foot high ornamental iron fence was affordable. When the first stretch of fence was ordered, I asked the salesman how far I needed to clear

Fences don't always have to be the standard vertical board on board style—this tall flared stake fence with a curved top makes its own contribution at the back of the garden, while a lower fence in the same style provides support for the pale pink rose 'Kathleen'.

GOING VERTICAL

Trellises, arbors and vertical planters allow you to move your plants up, conserving valuable ground. They can mask the air conditioner, screen the neighbor's garbage cans, and create a sense of privacy in spaces too small to accommodate shrubs.

Start by identifying potential growing space and support structures. You can purchase a trellis, arbor or other type of support or get creative and make your own. Some of the best plant supports are made from recycled items.

Whether commercial or homemade, your structure must be able to support the weight of the plant. Wisteria, bittersweet and a few other vines have pulled trellises off the wall and knocked them to the ground.

Make sure the structure is suited for the vines you are growing. Twining vines like clematis and akebia need something to twine around. Euonymus and climbing hydrangea need a rough surface to cling to.

Also consider maintenance of the support structure and the building it is mounted upon. You must be able to access your house for painting, installing screens and other yearly tasks. Some gardeners use hinged trellises to accomplish this. The trellises are hinged at ground level and use a hook to attach to an eyebolt in the wall. The trellis, vine and all, can be carefully laid down and out of the way when painting or otherwise maintaining your house.

Do not train vines onto wood-sided houses. The vines trap moisture next to the siding causing the siding to deteriorate. The rootlets and holdfasts can physically damage the siding as well. Avoid using vines on aluminum and vinyl siding. Many vines leave a telltale stain years after they were removed. Place a trellis next to the house to grow attractive vines without sacrificing the beauty and well-being of your home.

With some creativity, fences can reflect the style and mood of their surroundings—this logpole fence in southwestern Colorado is perfect for its surroundings.

the plants for the installation. He said I would want to permanently keep my plants three feet away from the fence. When I asked why, he replied "You don't want to cover up your beautiful fence with plants!" Little did he know I considered my fence one big trellis for climbing vines and a pretty backdrop for my perennials and shrubs.

Solid or chain link fences or a wall of the garage or your home may also be a part of your small space garden. Use wall-mounted planters, vines, hanging baskets and garden art to soften or even hide the fence. Create a garden wall with lumber, black plastic and chicken wire or lattice. Chicago Botanic Garden has several on display in the Buehler Enabling Garden, a garden designed to show that people of any age and any physical challenge can still enjoy gardening. Use 2×4's to create a frame for the wall planter. Back it with plywood or sturdy weather resistant material. Use additional 2×4's to create smaller sections and supports within the overall frame. Remember the bigger the frame, the heavier the planter, and the more support needed.

Fill the planting sections with soil, cover with 4 to 6 mil black plastic, then plastic coated wire mesh, and finally lattice or similar wood to hold the soil and plants in place. Screw the top layers in place allowing you to disassemble the planter for winter storage, spring cleaning, and a yearly change of soil. Cut openings in the plastic and as needed through the wire covering for planting. Mount the planter on the wall or fence for lots of color in very little space.

Wall planters, window boxes, even sections of gutter hanging on the wall can provide growing space where

Window boxes needn't be confined to windows—this one, positioned on a wall between two windows, makes a stunning wall planter overflowing with coleus and variegated ivy.

This planter wall from the Chicago Botanic Garden can easily be reproduced in shapes and sizes to fit lots of gardens. As the plants grow they cover the mechanics of the planter.

you thought none existed. In addition, wall planters place the plants within easy reach for those with bad knees, arthritis, in wheelchairs or with other limitations that make bending difficult. Container gardens can do the same. Large potted tropicals and vines can soften a brick wall where there is no space available to plant. It's just like decorating the walls of your home.

In thinking about views, don't just consider your own. Take a walk on the outside of the fence or screen to check out what your neighbor is looking at. A small planting bed on the outside of the fence goes a long way to connect your landscape to the neighborhood, create an attractive divider, and maintain friendly relations with all involved. One central city gardener taught me this valuable lesson. He installed a fence for security but wanted to maintain a connection to his neighborhood. So, he left three feet on the outside of his fence to grow a garden for his neighbors to enjoy. It dressed up the alley and softened the neighbor's view.

Be sure to consider price and maintenance when selecting your screening materials. Make sure the materials will hold up to the rigors of your climate. If painting or other maintenance is required, how will that impact your plantings? Will vines need to be removed or shrubs covered when the fence is stained or painted? And how will plants impact the structure? Vines

This gardener has not only chosen a low fence that lets passers-by view the garden, but has also planted the space between the sidewalk and the street, giving neighbors even more enjoyment.

growing directly on a wood house or fence can lead to rot. A trellis with air space behind it mounted on a wood structure can provide color without damaging the siding. But you will need to deal with the trellis and plants when painting or staining the siding. Some gardeners use hinged frames that can be bent away from the house or fence when painting is needed. Others train vines on twine or wire supported by hooks or brackets mounted on the structure. These gardeners can unhook the support and move the plants out of the way, or simply prune back the vines, remove the wire and work around the hooks and brackets when home maintenance is needed.

A Room within a Room

Use smaller plants and low screening to further define areas within the garden. A section of fencing, a grouping of short ornamental grasses and perennials, or dwarf conifers and other features can create small areas with added privacy, a special view or a garden vignette to be enjoyed from another vantage point.

Use dividers to create transitions and delineate different styles and moods within your garden. A group of ornamental grasses fronted by colorful perennials may be just the divider needed to separate a solitary chaise lounge meant for reading or napping from the busier areas intended for eating and visiting with family and friends. Or maybe you would like to set apart the unique style and purpose of a Zen meditation garden from the surrounding small space garden.

Wattle fences crafted from branches pruned from your landscape are great ways to recycle yard waste and create attractive dividers. Sections of bamboo screening or of lattice, picket or iron fencing make effective and attractive dividers. Some gardeners build low walls of brick or stone to create room dividers and provide a backdrop for plants. Always keep in mind the overall garden design as well as the mood and look you are trying to achieve. More is not always better, and this is definitely the case with small space gardens. Too many styles and too much variety can create a feeling of chaos and make your small space garden seem even smaller.

CAN'T MISS TIP:

FAUX TREE

Create the illusion of a small tree by purchasing a shrub grafted onto a standard. The shrub top forms the canopy and the straight stem the shrub was grafted onto is the trunk. Prune the shrub top to shape and control the size of this small "tree."

Even large, unruly shrubs like forsythia can work in a small garden if they're trained as small trees.

WEAVE YOUR OWN WATTLE FENCE

Recycle your twigs and branches by creating rustic wattle fences. Use these for screening, fencing, dividers or edging. These woven fences have traditionally been made of hazel and willow, but any pliable branch will do.

- Select stout sturdy stems at least as long as the desired fence height plus one foot. Shape or prune the base into a point for easier installation.

- Push or pound the support stakes into the ground at least 8 inches deep or preferably deeper and 2 feet apart.

- Select long (the length of the fence) pliable branches to create the sides.

- Weave the pliable branches in front of one post, behind the next and continue alternating the length of the fence.

- Slide the first woven row to the bottom. Adjust so it is even across the bottom of the fence.

- Repeat, alternating the weaving so one row is under and the next row is over the support.

Low wattle fencing in this garden delineates raised beds used for strawberries, onions, and other edibles.

In no time you will have recycled your yard waste into an attractive and functional part of the garden.

Use plants for a softer division of space. A few tall plants in the middle of a garden can create the feel of two separate gardens when viewed from different vantage points. Plants like moor grass are perfect candidates for this role. This ornamental grass produces a 2- to 3-foot tall rosette of foliage topped by an airy covering of flowers that can reach 6 or more feet tall.

A low hedge of yew divides one garden area from another and is a great backdrop for an unusual bench and a showy pair of planters.

The airy top is like sheer curtains softening the view beyond. This grass, like other plants used as dividers, changes throughout the season, the year and over time. This provides added interest to your small space. Increase the impact of narrow beds by cresting the bed in the middle. The slight change in elevation increases the visual impact.

A Little Taste in the Middle

The space between the canopy and groundcover gives lots of opportunity to incorporate color and texture in the garden. Vines and planters on walls and fences, dividers providing rhythm and form, and all the annuals, bulbs and perennials that fill our traditional gardens add exactly that. But with some creativity, we can create a garden within our garden by carving out a little space for a pocket herb or vegetable garden. Or, you can try my approach of mixing edibles with the ornamental flowers and shrubs. You may decide to use raspberries as a hedge or espaliered apples as a screen so you have something edible as well as functional and beautiful. Rhubarb makes a great temporary shrub, and the colorful foliage and stems of Swiss chard add interest to any garden.

A friend of mine created an edible garden at her front entrance. She used Brussels sprouts as a vertical accent, nasturtium for its edible foliage and flowers, with Swiss chard and a bit of parsley for an edging. Salvia and alyssum were added for a bit of color and fragrance. It was fun to reach out and harvest fresh vegetables for our dinner.

Select family favorites and look for varieties with fragrance, texture, and colors that complement the rest of your design. Many of the new eggplants, peppers, tomatoes, and greens are being selected for their ornamental value as well as their flavor. A master gardener I know replaced a missing fence with pole beans. Consider scarlet runner beans for added color from the flowers and fruit. Or create a fence by pruning and training dwarf apples, pears and other tree fruits into an attractive fence. You will need some sturdy posts, wires and a pair of sharp pruning shears. The goal is to train branches into a narrow divider. I have seen branches crisscrossed and wired to form decorative patterns. You can also use the same technique to train fruit and ornamental trees and shrubs flat against a fence or wall.

A low fence divides one garden room from another and creates a courtyard—the shrubs on the house walls will create a real challenge when time comes to paint the siding.

This is a great way to create an edible screen or divider for your garden.

And don't forget the herbs. Their fragrance, texture and often colorful foliage add interest to the garden. Purple ruffles basil is a great container and bedding plant. The colorful foliage contrasts nicely with yellows in the garden. Or plant it with tricolor sage and eggplant to bring out the purple in other plants. Thyme, lavender and rosemary all add texture and fragrance to any ornamental or edible garden. Even those of you who hate cooking may find a place for herbs in your garden— I did. One of my neighbors was sure I was a dynamite cook based on all the herbs I grew in my garden. Nothing could be further from the truth—I cook because we need to eat. But I do find growing my own herbs and vegetables makes the process a bit less painful and the end result much tastier.

Basil, dill, Swiss chard and apples all mingle beautifully in this tiny garden, guarded by a topiary bunny guaranteed not to eat the goodies.

The Floor

Last but not least is the groundcover layer. Consider how you will be using the space when selecting the floor covering. Hard surfaces such as pavers

Gravel makes an informal, inexpensive, and pleasantly crunchy groundcover, but it can be difficult to keep clear of leaves, ice, and snow.

Thyme and moss among the rocks are a lovely, low maintenance alternative to grass in this secluded garden with low walls of boxwood.

and flagstone are great for handling foot traffic and furniture. Gravel adds sound as you walk but is troublesome if you need to keep the walk clear of ice and snow or falling leaves. Make sure the material fits your landscape design, withstands the climate and works with your budget. I have met several industrious gardeners who recycled old street pavers into their gardens. They worked with their municipalities to collect and haul away the old pavers during street construction. These made great paths and fit perfectly with the landscape design and architecture of their older homes.

Loosely spaced flagstone with mulch in between creates an informal paving surface.

Grass is a favorite ground-cover of many gardeners, but getting a mower into a small space may not be possible. You may find you spend more time starting, storing and maintaining your mower than you do cutting the small patch of grass. Consider using groundcovers that provide more than green to your small plot of earth.

These low-growing plants provide a no-mow green alternative to grass. They cover the soil, helping to keep

GROUNDCOVERS

A few groundcovers for shade:

- **Bearberry** (*Artcostaphylos*) zones 2–8
- **Barrenwort** (*Epimedium*) zones 5–8
- **Bugleweed** (*Ajuga*) zones 3–9
- **Coral bells** (*Heuchera*) zones 3–8
- **Creeping mahonia** (*Mahonia repens*) zones 5–8
- **Creeping veronica** (*Veronica prostrata*) zones 5–8
- **Deadnettle** (*Lamium maculatum*) zones 4–8
- **English ivy** (*Hedera helix*) zones 4–9 invasive in some regions
- **Ginger, Canadian** (*Asarum canadensis*) zones 2–8

- **Ginger, European** (*Asarum europeum*) zones 4–9
- **Golden moneywort** (*Lysimachia nummularia* 'Aurea') zones 4–8
- **Hosta** (*Hosta* species) zones 3–8
- **Lilyturf** (*Liriope*) zones 5–11
- **Pachysandra** (*Pachysandra terminalis*) zones 4–8
- **Periwinkle** (*Vinca minor*) zones 4–9 invasive in some locations
- **Sweet woodruff** (*Galium odorata*) zones 5–8
- **Wintercreeper** (*Euonymus fortunei* cultivars) zones 4–9 some are invasive in some regions

A few groundcovers for full sun and dry locations:

- **Blue fescue** (*Festuca glauca*) zones 4–8
- **Catmint** (*Nepeta faassennii*) zones 4–8
- **Creeping juniper** (*Juniperus*) zones 3–9
- **Creeping phlox** (*Phlox*) zones 3–8
- **Hens and chicks** (*Sempervivum tectorum*) zones 4–8
- **Ice plant** (*Delosperma nubigerum*) zones 6–9

- **Lamb's ear** (*Stachys byzantina*) zones 4–8
- **Rock rose** (*Cistus*) zones 8–10
- **Snow-in-summer** (*Cerastium tomentosum*) zones 3–7
- **Stonecrop** (*Sedum*) zones 3–10
- **Thyme** (*Thymus* species) zones 4–9

*Hardiness varies with individual species

CAN'T MISS TIP:

STEPPABLES

Add some fragrant thyme or sweet alyssum in between steppers to create a fragrant walkway. As you and your visitors walk over the path, you all will be pleasantly surprised with a little aromatherapy.

weeds at bay, serve as a natural air conditioner cooling the surrounding area, and protect the soil from erosion. Many are evergreen, and some have flowers while others provide a colorful show in fall. Select drought-tolerant groundcover plants for drier climates and moisture lovers for wet areas, then match the light requirements to the site. I like to create a tapestry by using a variety of groundcovers. A mix of coral bells, hostas, lungwort, brunnera, bergenia, Canadian ginger and astilbe give me some color and a mosaic of green throughout the season.

Mix hard surfaces with groundcovers. A patio or small circle of pavers can provide the solid surface needed for your umbrella stand. Surround it with plants to soften the hard surface and anchor it to the landscape.

Try shade-tolerant groundcovers such as deadnettle and moneywort for shady areas. One gardener used golden moneywort as a groundcover in her shade garden. Its lime green foliage made the green leaves of hosta, ginger and other shade lovers just pop. And stop fighting the moss in those heavy shaded areas where even shade-tolerant groundcovers won't grow. Add a few flagstones to the moss-covered ground, and you have a moss garden that will be the envy of your family and friends.

You can also use plants to cover the aging surface of an old patio. Try planting small transplants or seeds in the cracks and openings. You may need to widen some of the narrow cracks or even add a few more to increase planting space. Either use plants that can tolerate an occasional stray step or position plants out of the main thoroughfare to avoid damage.

As you start shopping for groundcovers, remember light conditions change in your small garden every time you add a vine-covered arbor, small tree or other shade-producing feature. And where there is shade there is often a shortage of moisture. The solid cover of an awning or the dense canopy of a shade tree can prevent water from reaching the plants in the ground below. Plus nearby plants will compete with the groundcover for the water that does make it to the ground. Select plants tolerant of your light, soil and moisture conditions. You will need to water new plantings (even of drought-tolerant plants) until they are established and better able to compete with surrounding trees and shrubs.

Accents

Now that you have the foundation and bones of the garden figured out, it's time to add a few accents. Look toward showy annuals for season-long color. Include a few perennials to provide subtle interest and dramatic changes at times during the season. Create mixed beds filled with bulbs, annuals and perennials for year-round interest. Select a pot and add a few blooming beauties to areas where there is no soil for planting (more on this in chapter 4).

You can pack in more plants and create the feel of a larger garden by doubling up on your planting. Mix bulbs with your perennials and flowers with your shrubs. This way you have several different plants in the same location providing year-round seasonal interest. Variety can add a little spice

LIVEN UP AN OLD CEMENT SURFACE

Replacing an out-dated, cracked or stained cement patio can be expensive. Bringing one back to life or covering it up can transform an eyesore into an asset.

- **Paint or stain it.** Paints and stains are available to help add color, cover stains and liven up an old concrete slab. Stains can improve the appearance and add color to the cement. However, they can't completely cover another color. Use paint if you want to cover an old paint job or create a multicolored pattern, picture or mosaic on your patio. Check with your local hardware store for help selecting the right product. Here are some things to remember:

  - **Clean the surface according to directions and allow it to thoroughly dry prior to painting.** Some cleaning products are harmful to plants. You may need to cover or temporarily move nearby plants to avoid damage.

  - **Select a product with UV color protection** if the patio receives lots of sun.

  - **Ask about the surface.** Some cement paints are slippery when wet. You may need to add sand for traction if you plan on walking across the patio when wet.

- **Be patient.** These products require more drying time between coats and prior to use than wall paints. Your patience will give you better looking results.

- **Cover it with a deck.** Make your own or purchase prefabricated modular wood decking to cover your old patio. My friend built small deck sections mounted on 2 x 4's. He set them on top of an old patio for a newer look. Those of us less handy gardeners can purchase interlocking deck tiles or modular deck sections for just this purpose.

- **Cover the surface with pea gravel.** Gravel topping can update the look, provide sound and a bit of motion when walking. Add a few steppers to create a solid surface for furniture and walking. Evaluate the impact of fall leaves and snow on the use and cleanup of this surface before purchasing the materials.

FLOORING FOR THE BALCONY

Stepping out of your living space onto a lawn might be nice but that isn't the most practical choice for your balcony. Consider one of these alternatives:

- Indoor outdoor carpeting is not what it used to be—it is much better. You will be amazed at the quality and colors available. I have a neutral carpet covering the metal surface of my balcony. It has spent two summers and one Wisconsin winter outdoors and still looks brand new.

- Straw mats can provide texture and color to your balcony floor. Use several colors to create an interesting pattern or just one for a more subdued effect. Make sure the texture, color and design complement the furnishings.

- Try using wood deck tiles or floating deck.

to the garden as well as to your life. Plus diversifying your plantings helps reduce disease and insect problems.

I love to mix bulbs in with groundcovers. One of my favorite plant combinations is autumn crocus planted amid vinca, wintercreeper or another low-growing groundcover. The autumn crocus leaves sprout in March or April, grow for a month or so and die back. The groundcover grows, flowers, and looks good all summer. Then in fall, the leafless autumn crocus flowers peek through the greenery. It looks like the groundcover is blooming but this time with crocus flowers.

Pansies and bulbs make another nice space-saving combination. The pansies serve as a colorful groundcover around the properly spaced daffodils and tulips. As the bulbs' flowers pass and their foliage begins to fade, the pansies help mask their demise. Plant pansies in fall for a colorful display in fall, winter (you lucky southern gardeners!) and spring. Northern gardeners should use cold hardy cultivars such as 'Icicle', 'Sub-Zero' and 'Second Season'. The pansies will be in place and ready to partner with the bulbs in spring. In summer replace the pansies with warm weather annuals such as petunias and begonias.

Ambitious gardeners may want to create greater interest with seasonal changes. Try pansies or snapdragons in the spring, followed by annual vinca or Dahlberg daisies in the summer, and mums or flowering kale for the fall. One of our local garden centers added ornamental mustard to the mix of fall choices. Winter can be the season of holiday greens in the north or hardy annuals in the south. You may have no more space but there certainly are additional ways to use what you have.

Then make sure each plant counts. You may not be able to add more planting space but you can strive to maximize the beauty in the limited

A cool-looking shade garden is accented with variegated ribbon grass amid cinnamon fern, euphorbia, heliotrope, and scilla—lots of plants packed into one tiny corner.

Left: This planting of 'Frosted Curls' sedge and sedum 'Autumn Joy' will make a contribution in three seasons—here, in late summer, the sedum's flower buds are just forming but the combination is already lovely.

Center: In early fall, the sedum blooms with its deep pink set off against the silver sedge.

Right: After the first frost, the sedum's blossoms have turned to coppery-red, its leaves have begun to yellow, and the sedge is looking frosty, but the combination is still striking. The seedheads and dried grass will add to the garden's winter appeal.

space available. Look for plants that provide several seasons, preferably four seasons, of interest. The serviceberry (*Amelanchier*) is a perfect example. It has white flowers in spring, edible blueberry-like fruit in June, yellow-orange-red fall color, and attractive smooth gray bark for winter.

I had to follow my own advice on this one. When I moved into my home, I was offered a lilac. I had a lilac at my childhood home and always wanted one right outside the bedroom window of my own home. As I looked around my small yard, I realized the lilac would be great in bloom but boring the rest of the year, and I just didn't have enough space for one-season plants.

CAN'T MISS TIP:

STONE ACCENTS

Boulders are great accents in any size garden. They make a nice backdrop for flowers, a warming stone for butterflies, and a seat for family and friends. Plant, don't roll, your boulder in place to give it a natural look. In nature you see boulders erupting from the ground. So bury the bottom portion or surround it with plants to anchor your boulder to the garden.

So I passed on the lilac and bought a serviceberry. Besides, my bedroom is on the second floor.

Once your plants are selected, you will want to plan for a few more features to add to the beauty and increase your enjoyment of your outdoor living space. Artwork, water features, and furniture can complement your garden's design and provide added enjoyment.

Garden statuary, just like any structure, can

complement or detract from your overall design. Select artwork for your garden the same way you would for your home. Consider the overall design, color scheme, and value the artwork provides. Then find a suitable place for the piece so it can be viewed and enjoyed. Use plants to connect the artwork or statue to the rest of the landscape. Often garden art is set in the middle of lawn as if the owner had no idea what to do with an unwelcome gift. Look for plants that complement the color or theme of the work. The plants will help connect the statue to the rest of the design.

Furniture is another feature to be carefully considered. We have so many more options today than the wooden picnic tables and webbed lawn chairs of my childhood. As more gardeners downsize to condos and apartments or create small outdoor living spaces within their larger landscapes, companies are designing and producing furniture to meet these special garden needs. New features have been added to outdoor furniture to enhance its use in small spaces. Many garden benches come with hidden storage bins built under the seat, and collapsible chairs with side pockets for reading materials and cup holders for beverages fold up for easy storage when not in use. Materials include everything from teak, to colorful plastic lumber, to fiberglass, to canvas, to metal. Check out retail outlets and garden centers specializing in outdoor furnishings, catalogues and the Internet to see which products best suit your needs and your space.

This witty placement of the statue of a woman under a rose-covered arbor makes good use of both the statuary and the arbor.

The blue wicker furniture was the perfect choice for this small, lush entry garden.

This rustic, Adirondack-styled furniture is a good match for the informal garden and rustic fence.

CAN'T MISS TIP:

ACCESSORIZE CAREFULLY

As you select accessories for your garden, keep in mind that repetition of materials helps give a garden a sense of unity. You might have all wooden furniture, all terra cotta pots, or all stone statuary.

As you shop for furniture check out other accessories designed for outdoor living spaces. Music lovers may want to bring their favorite tunes into the garden using wireless speakers or those hidden in fake boulders or other decorative features. Decorative table and floor lamps, miniature grills, weather-resistant game boards, and other accessories help create a cozy enjoyable space.

Water, Water Everywhere

Water is another feature that can help us enjoy our outdoor living space. The sound of water can be soothing, mask nearby traffic and city noise, and attract birds and butterflies to the garden. I opted for a wall-mounted fountain for my upstairs balcony. I did not want to sacrifice any floor space, and I wanted something very low maintenance. The lightweight fiberglass fountain matched the lannon stone trim on my house. It was easy to mount and hangs on the outside wall of my brick home. Mine plugs into an electrical outlet but solar pumps are also available. The water drips from a spout and recirculates through the fountain, creating a soothing sound that I can even hear down below when working in my back garden. And on several occasions, I have been joined by a robin that stopped by for a drink.

Dripping stones, leaking crocks and other small-scale fountains are perfect for small spaces. The small footprint of the structure teamed with minimal space needed for the mechanics allow gardeners with even the tiniest spaces to add water to their landscapes. I also like the low level of maintenance required for these types of features.

Real water gardens, complete with fish and plants, are also an option. Attractive ceramic pots, lined whiskey barrels, and troughs allow gardeners to grow water plants in limited quarters. These are great ways to "test the waters" and see if water gardening fits into your schedule. People with enough garden space to spare may want to try a small pool. Prefabricated liners come in a variety of sizes. I visited one back yard that included a small stream running alongside the fence. Though small in size, it fit the scale of the city lot, attracted birds and provided the aesthetics the owner desired.

Do your homework before digging the hole for your water feature. Check with your municipality regarding regulations on depth and on fencing requirements. Look for a level piece of ground that does not collect water from the surrounding lawn and gardens, since this runoff may contain chemicals harmful to plants and fish. Try to find a sunny spot that receives at least six hours of sun to give you the greatest choice of flowering plants. Avoid placing the water garden under shade trees whose shade and falling leaves will increase algae problems and create more clean-up for you. Plan for the additional space needed to hide the power source, pump and other mechanics needed to operate and maintain a water garden.

A well-planned garden with the right mix of plants and fish can provide lots of beauty with minimal care. Northern gardeners will need to take some special steps for winter.

Tropical plants will need to be over-wintered indoors or replaced each spring. Fish will need a winter home indoors, open water, or a pond deep enough that it does not freeze solid in winter. Some gardeners use water-

CAN'T MISS
TIP:

WILDLIFE

Even in an urban setting, you'll be surprised by how quickly wildlife finds and takes up residence in your pond. Frogs, especially, seem to appear overnight. And moving water will do more to attract birds than bird feeders do.

A small cherub fountain pouring into a low moss-covered basin makes a beautiful feature in a small, shady space.

If there's no room for an in-ground pond, try a plastic lined whiskey barrel and an old-fashioned water pump with a few plants.

ing troughs under lights in the basement to over-winter their tropical lilies and fish. Others use heaters to keep the water open for the fish and visiting birds. And one friend buys small goldfish every spring from the pet shop to enjoy all summer in her small pond. She returns them in fall for a small credit and applies it to her purchase the following spring.

Avoid problems by consulting the water gardening experts at garden centers and aquatic nurseries. It may be cheaper in the long run to consult an expert rather than replace incorrect purchases, fight algae problems due to an unbalanced ecosystem and patch leaks. A bit of advice and reading in advance will help determine the best course of action for designing, installing and maintaining your pond.

Designing with Plants

Don't worry if you have not been successful with gardening in the past. Like your small space garden, a green thumb and design skills will grow over time. If you are an experienced gardener, the planning process will help hone your garden design skills. Together we will work to minimize mistakes and increase success when planning, planting and caring for your small space garden.

Creating a beautiful garden starts by selecting the right plant for the location. But a garden is more than just a collection of plants. Like many plant lovers, I have created a botanical zoo. Our landscapes are filled with one or two specimens of many varieties of plants. We have "drifts of one" plant that allow us to squeeze lots of variety into not much space. A diverse collection of plants can soothe the plant collector's addiction but it also adds challenge to designing and maintaining the landscape.

It requires a bit more effort to create a sense of unity in a garden with such a wide array of plants. And if your collection grows so large you need help maintaining it, you may find it hard to locate a qualified person or willing friend to lend a hand. I know, it happened to me. I had one too many busy summers and needed some help getting the weeds under control, so I hired my friend's landscape crew to help me for a day. They arrived with hedge shears and edgers ready to go to work. I think they were disappointed when I announced we, me included, were going to spend the day on our hands and knees weeding. I showed them the three major weeds and instructed them to talk to me before pulling anything else. Can you imagine the stories back at their shop? "You think you had a bad day? Well, I spent mine weeding on my hands and knees, and the homeowner was right by my side." It turned out fine but taught me to keep up with maintenance since I can't seem to part with my collection of plants.

Whether your garden is large or small, you can create greater impact and reduce maintenance by using fewer species of plants and more of each one. Identifying ten perennials is much easier than trying to remember if that plant in the corner is something you planted or a weed that wandered in on its own. Trust me, I have weeded out a few perennials and nourished a few weeds in my own garden.

Planting in drifts of three, five, or even seven of the same plant can increase the impact of their foliage, flowers, fall color or winter interest without increasing the maintenance. These plants all will need the same type of care at the same time. So if you are feeling a bit overwhelmed or limited as to time, you may want to start with fewer types of plants for greater impact with less effort. No matter what strategy you use, remember all green-thumbed gardeners make mistakes and replace or move their fair share of plants.

Gardens featuring only one of each of several plants can look a bit spotty in their effect, especially when they're flowering plants in hot colors.

Right Plant in the Right Place

A beautiful garden is only as pretty as the plants it contains. And those plants are only pretty when they are healthy and growing in the right location. Make sure the plants you select will fit their growing space when mature and will thrive in the existing conditions.

Most gardeners are guilty of using the shoehorn planting technique. We squeeze one or maybe even two extra plants into the available planting space even though experience has taught us these extra plants can become a liability. Overcrowding can lead to disease, stunted growth and poor flowering. We end up thinning the planting and either composting the extra plants or moving them to another location, perhaps a friend's or neighbor's yard. These lucky recipients will be disappointed when you start planning for the available space and stop passing along your excess purchases for their landscapes. But for you, this will mean more money to spend on garden accessories and other embellishments for your new small garden.

Use the landscape templates on page 166 to help determine placement and spacing of plants, containers and other landscape features. It is much

LOOK UP TO PLANT

Even the sky is not the limit when it comes to gardeners. Many have converted once vacant rooftops to green oases in the city. This common practice in Europe is finding its way across the ocean. Rooftops once covered with asphalt and tar are now covered with grass, a few containers, or maybe even a landscape complete with lawn.

The goal of this planting system is to capture rainwater, utilize the water for plant growth, and filter it through the planting system. Green roof systems reduce storm water runoff while cutting heating and cooling costs

Anything is possible, but you do need to do your homework before you rent the crane and equipment to move soil, trees and shrubs to the roof. Make sure the roof can handle the added weight of soil, plants, and the people who may be using the space. Consult with a licensed engineer.

The next call needs to go to your local municipality. Check on any ordinances or building codes that may restrict or guide your building process. Time and energy spent now may mean the difference between enjoying a rooftop garden and spending the time removing all your hard work.

See **www.greenroofs.net** for more information.

CHOOSING EVERGREENS

Evergreen shrubs such as junipers, yews, false cypress, and arborvitaes add year-round interest to the garden. Some old favorites and new cultivars have unique foliage texture and color. Many have more contained growth or better longevity in the landscape and deserve a second look. But check the label for mature size on these plants. Those cute little evergreens can quickly become giants that overrun your small garden.

Use pines and spruces in full sun. These are drought-tolerant and good choices for dry locations. Chamaecyparis (false cypress), yews, hemlocks and arborvitae can be grown in full sun or light shade but prefer moist soils. They all, especially the hemlocks and chamaecyparis, do best when protected from drying winds. And hemlocks are very shade tolerant.

So let's look at how to incorporate miniature and dwarf conifers into your small garden. Group dwarf conifers of varying colors, textures and shapes to create year-round anchors in the garden. Add a few perennials, bulbs or annuals, and you have interesting vignettes that change from season to season and year to year.

Start with some simple combinations such as cranberry cotoneaster and steely blue juniper as a groundcover. Or maybe try a dwarf mugo pine, a golden upright arborvitae, and a yellow daylily. Tie this trio together with a groundcover tapestry of lady's mantle and sweet woodruff, add a little punch with 'Plum Pudding' or one of the other purple-leafed coral bells, and you have extended bloom, fragrance and year-round interest.

This dwarf blue spruce makes a big impact nestled between an oakleaf hydrangea in back and variegated iris in front.

Use some of the small vertical conifers to create a focal point or give the feel of depth in a small bed. Look for upright plants with a small footprint. These will give you height without sacrificing planting space. A dwarf Alberta spruce, a small upright arborvitae, a juniper or a false cypress combined with a variegated ornamental grass, a blue hosta (for part shade) or *Salvia argentea* or lamb's ear (hot sun) make an effective season-long foliar display.

DWARF CONIFERS

Common Name / (Botanical Name) / Hardiness / Height in 10 years / (*ACS category) / Comment

Silverlock Korean fir / (*Abies koreana* 'Silberlocke') / zone 5 / 4 feet in 10 years / (I) / Pyramidal plants with green needles that twist to reveal silvery underside, prefers afternoon shade.

Nootka false cypress / *Chamaecyparis nootkatensis* 'Pendula' / zone 5 / 6 to 7 feet in 10 years / (L) / Drooping branchlets of this weeping tree form make it a graceful addition to the landcape. 'Green Arrow' is an even narrower weeping form.

Hinoki false cypress / *Chamaecyparis obtusa* 'Nana Gracilis' / zone 5 / 3 feet in 10 years / (D) / Texture, dark green foliage, benefits from protection, globose becoming upright, tolerates light shade.

Mops sawara
Chamaecyparis pisifera 'Golden Mop' / zone 4 / 3 ft in 10 years / (D) / Also called mops, bright gold threadlike foliage, mounded.
C. p. 'Filifera Aurea Nana' / zone 4 / 3 ft in 10 yrs / (D) / Mounded to widely pyramidal, threadlike foliage with golden tips.
C. p. 'Filifera Aureovariegata' / zone 4 / 3 feet in 10 years / (D) / Threadlike foliage with creamy tips, mounded.
Chamaecyparis in general provide nice texture, various forms.

Bird's nest spruce
Picea abies 'Nidiformis' /zone 3 / 3 feet in 10 years / (D) / Spreading/mounded growth habit—great in rock gardens and perennial gardens.
P. a. 'Elegans' / zone 3 / 3 feet in 10 years / (D) / Similar to 'Nidiformis' but superior appearance though more difficult to find.

Dwarf Alberta spruce
Picea glauca 'Conica' / zone 3 / 3.5 feet in 10 years / (D) / Perfect pyramid with dense growth and soft texture, protect from winter wind and sun.
P. g. 'Rainbow's End' / zone 3 / 4 feet in 10 years / (D) / Dwarf Alberta with flush of creamy new growth.
P.g. 'Sander's Blue' / zone 3 / 3 feet in 10 years / (D) / Dwarf Alberta that starts out very blue and then becomes mix of green and blue.

Fat Albert blue spruce / *Picea pungens* 'Fat Albert' / Zone 3 / 5 feet in 10 years / (I) / A chubby pyramidal spruce with good blue color.

Dwarf blue spruce / *Picea pungens* 'Montgomery' / zone 3 / 3 feet in 10 years / (D) / A dense mound of blue needles. This dwarf Colorado blue spruce becomes pyramidal with age.

Dwarf mugo pine
Pinus mugo 'Mops' / zone 3 / 2 feet in 10 years / (D) / A dwarf mugo with globose form that grows as tall as wide, one of the better mugos.
P. m. 'Aurea' / zone 2 / 3 feet in 10 years / (D) / Needles on this mugo turn gold for winter.
P. m. 'Sherwood Compact' / zone 2 / 2 feet in 10 years / (D) / Dark green needles form a uniform dense mound.

Korean arborvitae / *Thuja koraiensis* 'Glauca Prostrata' / zone 4 / 4 feet in 10 years / (D) / This low-growing, spreading form and white undersides on the scales gives it big appeal for its small size. Prefers full sun but tolerates shade.

American arborvitae / *Thuja occidentalis* / many sizes, shapes and variegated cultivars available

Dwarf eastern arborvitae
Thuja occidentalis 'Holmstrup' / zone 4 / 3 feet in 10 years / (D to I) / Narrow upright and shorter arborvitae often classes as intermediate.
T. o. 'Technito'™ / zone 4 / 4 feet in 10 (D to I) / A shorter version with dense pyramidal habit.

Golden western arborvitae
Thuja occidentalis 'Reingold' / zone 4 / 3 feet in 10 years / (D) / A globose form with golden-orange foliage year-round.
T.o. 'Sunkist' / zone 4 / 4 feet / (I) / Intermediate

Prostrate Canadian hemlock
Tsuga canadensis 'Cole' / zone 4 / 2.5 feet in 10 years / (D) / Dark green needles on low and spreading plant makes a great groundcover. Shade tolerant.
T. c. 'Gentsch White' / zone 4 / 3 feet in 10 years / (D) / This shade-tolerant evergreen has a globose to widely pyramidal form. The new growth is white tipped.

*ACS - American Conifer Society

easier to move the templates around on paper than it is to dig and move plants or reinstall a misplaced arbor.

With a small garden you also need to think about small plants. That doesn't mean just annuals and perennials but also small trees, shrubs and evergreens. Fortunately, many breeders are giving us a hand by developing and introducing new dwarf varieties. As we mentioned in Chapter 1, even if a plant's label says dwarf, you need to check its ultimate size before buying and planting it in the yard. The preface "dwarf" only means it is smaller than the standard plant.

If you own a dwarf mugo pine or burning bush you know what I mean. You, like most gardeners, probably bought these "dwarf" plants and placed them below your front windows. In a few years, they grew up and beyond the window, blocking the view. You probably had to remove the overgrown mugo pine and are still pruning the euonymus each year to maintain the view. Not what you had planned. So avoid the problem by selecting plants with the desired mature size.

Another area of amazing market expansion is in the selection of dwarf conifers (cone-bearing plants). These include smaller versions of familiar giants such as spruce, pine, cedar, false cypress, arborvitae and juniper. The wide variety of sizes, shapes and even colors can be overwhelming. And just as with other plants, dwarf only means smaller than the standard size. So I like to use the American Conifer Society (ACS) classification system to help me select the right conifer for the garden.

ACS classifies conifers by growth rate and approximate size at 10 years of age. A miniature conifer grows less than 1 inch per year and is less than a foot tall after 10 years. A dwarf grows 1 to 6 inches each year and is 1 to 6 feet tall after 10 years. An intermediate is larger and faster-growing with a 6 to 12 inch per year growth rate and 6 to 15 feet height in 10 years. Anything faster-growing or bigger is classed as a large conifer—you know, like that Colorado blue spruce that engulfed the front entrance after 15 years in the landscape.

Size is only one consideration. Select plants suited to the growing conditions in your region and your garden. Plants adapted to the environment will flourish with minimal care and develop into beautiful assets in your garden. Growing conditions were covered in more detail in Chapter 1, and you collected information specific to your site. Refer to these notes when selecting plants for your garden. The plant lists in this chapter include some basic information, while more details are included for selected good small space plants in Chapter 5.

Select plants suited to the growing conditions in your region and your garden.

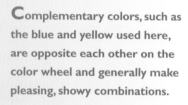

Related colors, those that are either next to or nearby each other on the color wheel, work well together—in this case the airy red blooms, blue grass, and purple catmint make a lovely combo.

Complementary colors, such as the blue and yellow used here, are opposite each other on the color wheel and generally make pleasing, showy combinations.

Color It Up

Use color to create unity, balance and interest in your garden. The colors you choose can create a mood and help achieve the look you desire. A color wheel is included on page 167 to make this part of the design process a bit easier.

Warm colors of red, yellow and orange grab attention. One or two warm-colored flowers can easily steal the show. My small front garden is filled with a variety of unusual plants, but it's the yellow black-eyed Susan that is the star each fall.

Use warm colors to create a focal point and add energy to your garden. They can also make a cool location seem warmer. Use warm and bright colors for festive areas in the garden. Or use them to bring boundaries closer. In long narrow spaces, warm colors can help even out the appearance of an uneven space. But be careful not to overuse these powerful colors and make your already small space feel even smaller.

Red supposedly increases the appetite, so dieters may want to avoid lots of red flowers mulched with cocoa bean shells. The hunger pangs and smell of chocolate just might lead to falling off the diet.

Blue, green and violet are cool colors. Include these to make your small space feel larger and to visually cool down a hot sunny space. You will need more cool flowers to create the same impact as just a few red, orange or yellow flowers. Begin observing what colors you notice first when viewing gardens, reading advertisements or driving along the freeway, and you'll find the warm colors are the attention-grabbers. But subtle colors can be used to create a relaxing, peaceful space.

White, like most of our mothers told us, goes with everything. Take a look in the garden and you will see mom was right. White can bridge a variety of colors, brighten the shade or evening garden and create a soothing mood.

Use complementary colors, those that are opposite each other on the color wheel, to create a focal point. These make strong but classic and appealing combinations in the garden. Visualize some of your favorites—blue with yellow or red with green.

Create a harmonious feel by using related colors. These are colors that appear next to each other on the color wheel. Related colors give variety as they build on one another to create a strong impact in the garden.

A monochromatic garden uses flowers and foliage of different shades and tones of one basic color. The shared color creates unity and impact in the garden. You are probably familiar with evening gardens filled with plants that have white flowers and silvery white foliage. This style is often used in classic and formal garden designs.

Use the color wheel to help you get a sense of color combinations that work. Make a paper triangle large enough so one corner just touches the yellow bar, one the red bar, and the last one the blue bar on the color wheel. This combination of the three primary colors is always a winner. As you turn the triangle around in the center of the color wheel each corner points to a different color. These three colors always make an attractive color combination to use in the garden

This is just a starting point. Every gardener knows that guidelines are meant to be adapted to your own preference and gardening style. And a quick look at nature will show you

CAN'T MISS TIP:

CHOOSING COLORS

One way to blend the indoors with the outdoors and make both appear larger is to let the colors in one inspire the colors in the other. It's especially effective to have a front garden that incorporates the colors of the entry hall, or for views from a given room into the garden to include the same color palette.

Avoid dark blue, purple or black flowers in shade areas. These dark colors recede into the foliage and background. Instead combine with yellow or back with silver foliage plants to make these colors pop.

You can think of your garden as a flower arrangement.

how she breaks the rules for some pretty outstanding colorful displays. Keep in mind that color combinations change throughout the year. Seasonal flower displays, fall foliage, fruit and colorful bark provide an ever changing palette of color in the garden. So if some of your plants aren't working together, just wait, they might be the perfect combination in another season.

Color Echoes

No, color echoes don't mean you have to shout out your favorite color from your second-story balcony and wait for it to bounce back off your neighbors' homes. Color echoing is a useful technique of repeating color throughout the landscape to create a sense of unity. So instead of making every third flower a red geranium we might have a group of red geraniums in one location, some red leafed amaranth in another section, and a red fruited cotoneaster in a nearby bed. The repetition of the various shades of red on different plants and different plant parts help tie all the elements of the garden together creating unity and balance.

This is a great technique for those of us with botanical zoos. The repetition of color in various plant parts and landscape features allows us to use a diversity of plants yet provide the feel of a cohesive garden. Take a look at the planting combinations that work in yours and others' gardens. You might be surprised to see color echoes already happening. With added attention, you can use this strategy to strengthen your landscape designs.

Bold and Beautiful or Fine and Fluffy

Like color, plant texture can do a lot to create a mood, add interest, and build unity and balance into the garden. Fine-textured plants tend to have spiky or airy flowers and narrow, often grass-like leaves. You need lots of these to have the same impact as one bold peony blossom.

Bold flowers are round and usually have wide leaves like hostas. These, like warm colors, grab the viewer's attention and tend to steal the show. You only need a few bold flowers to create a focal point in your small space garden.

You can think of your garden as a flower arrangement. A florist surrounds one bold rose blossom with the fine textured baby's breath. One without the other is pretty, but together they make a memorable combination. In fact, many designers start their garden designs in a vase. They collect a variety of flowers and foliage. They arrange them in a vase. If they look good in a vase they will probably look good in the garden. Just make sure all the plants you choose have the same growing requirements, are equally assertive and are arranged so the tall ones don't block the view of their shorter partners.

Combinations with Added Value

As you design your garden, keep all its aspects in mind. Boulders, statutes, flowers, shrubs, evergreens, and trees combine to make a beautiful landscape design. Observe how the form, color and texture of each complement the others. Keep in mind the scene will vary from season to season, making garden design a bit challenging but all the more exciting and rewarding.

As you select your plants, make sure they provide maximum value for the space they occupy. Select plants with four seasons of interest such as shrub roses with season-long bloom and rose hips for winter display or dwarf evergreens that serve as a year-round anchor and provide winter color in northern garden. You may want to include such plants as coneflowers for the finches, serviceberries for the cedar wax wings, verbena for the hummingbirds, and butterfly weed for the monarchs. Plants that give several seasons of interest, provide food and shelter for the birds or nectar for the butterflies, and are beautiful in and of themselves make every square inch of your small space garden colorful, interesting and entertaining.

So take a deep breath and get to work designing your garden. The good news is that you really can't go wrong. All plants provide some beauty and value, and most can be easily moved if you plant them in the wrong place. Every gardener has stumbled by accident onto the perfect plant combination or planned one that turned out to be so bad it immediately had to be redesigned and replanted.

If you suffer garden design block take a walk through your neighborhood or local botanical garden. Jot down ideas and plant combinations you like and could use in your own garden. It is okay to borrow ideas and inspiration from others. As a landscape designer once told me, "None of us has original ideas; we just keep borrowing from each other and improving on what we see." It's time to create your own small space masterpiece.

If imagination fails you in designing a real garden, do a faux one instead—this *trompe l'oeuil* painting on the side of a garden shed couldn't be more delightful in its depiction of an orchard.

3

Maintaining Your Garden

Small space gardening is about making the most of every inch. It is also often about making the most of every minute you have available to manage and enjoy your garden. I love to work in my garden—it's great for my mind, body and soul. But like many of you, I don't have as much time as I would like to tend the garden. Plus the more time spent tending, the less time there is for sitting, relaxing and enjoying the garden's sights, sounds and fragrances.

Over the years, through personal experience and techniques shared by other professionals and devoted gardeners, I have found strategies to help maximize the effort I put forth in my garden. One of my neighbors said she couldn't figure out how I kept the small garden between my alley and the fence looking good. She never saw me tending the garden, but the continuous bloom was a joy to her and all my other alley neighbors.

My secrets were soil preparation, plant selection and mulch for weed control. I did spend a few hours in that garden here and there throughout the season. But a bit of pruning and clean-up in late winter, some weeding and mulching in the summer, fall raking of tree leaves that found their way into the garden, and some time harvesting flowers with the neighborhood kids was pretty much all that was required. This garden was intended to make me happy when going and coming from work, but it was mainly designed for my neighbors' enjoyment. Plus, as a small space gardener you know never to waste potential gardening space.

This chapter focuses on helping you build the small garden or green retreat that fits your maintenance abilities. Whether time, bad knees or inexperience limit your landscape management, I will give you some strategies and techniques to help. So let's start building your garden.

From the Ground Up

When every square inch above ground counts, the same holds true for the area beneath your feet. Creating a fertile foundation for your small garden will help you get the greatest impact from the available space.

Most yards, large or small, are not blessed with high quality soil. They are often filled with clay soil, rocks, unidentifiable debris left from construction, and who knows what else. This mess is often covered with 2 inches of "black dirt" and capped with a layer of sod. A few trees are plopped into the ground, and the new landscape is ready to grow. At least, that is, for a year or two.

Then the long term effects of infertile, badly drained soil and little garden preparation begin to show up as lawn disease, tree decline and overall poor plant establishment and growth. Investing in the ground beneath your feet will substantially increase the beauty, longevity and long-term benefits

of your above-ground investment. It also will save time in the long run—time spent struggling to keep plants alive or replacing the ones that didn't survive.

The first step is a soil test. Contact your local university or the Cooperative Extension Service for information on soil testing. Many extension offices have a soil testing lab or will recommend state-certified labs to do the job. Or look in the yellow pages under soil testing. Select a state-certified lab for the best possible results.

Collect the samples for your soil test carefully, following the directions the testing agency provides.

A soil test will tell you what is in your soil and what you need to add to grow healthy plants. This is good for the plants, the environment and your pocket book. Adding only what your plants need avoids over-fertilization that can interfere with plant growth and flowering as well as harm the environment. Excess nutrients can leach through the soil into our groundwater.

Take a soil test anytime the ground isn't frozen and you have not recently fertilized. You may want to take the soil test when you start the design process. The lab can test the soil, and the results will be returned before you finish your design. Then you can implement the recommendations as soon as the weather and your schedule permit. Add organic matter when preparing the soil. I like to start soil preparation in the fall when the weather is cooler and the soil is drier. Investing time then gives me a jump on the upcoming planting season. This is also a great time to add organic matter to the soil. Wait until planting to incorporate fast-release fertilizers. Otherwise these materials will leach out of the soil before the plants are in place to absorb and use the nutrients.

A Simple Home Test

Evaluate your soil type with a simple hand test. Grab a handful of soil and gently squeeze. Now run some of the soil between your thumb and index finger. If the ribbon of soil feels gritty, you have sandy soil. If it is sticky and holds together, you have a high percentage of clay.

Now check the drainage. Dig a hole about 1 foot deep and 1 foot in diameter. Fill it with water and wait. Record how fast the water drains out

of the hole. If water recedes about an inch an hour, your soil is well drained. If it takes longer, then your soil's drainage needs to be improved. If the water drains much more quickly, you may want to increase the water-holding capacity to reduce watering needs.

The good news is that whatever your soil type, you can improve it. You just need time and energy to transform less than ideal soil into something productive. And lucky for you, as a small space gardener, you only have square feet instead of acres of soil to amend.

The best soil improvement method is the same whether your soil is sandy or clay. Adding several inches of organic matter, such as peat moss, aged manure or compost, improves drainage in clay soils and increases the water-holding capacity in sandy soils. Dig or till 2 to 4 inches of organic matter into the top 8 to 12 inches of soil. This creates a well-drained root zone perfect for most plants.

Upper left: If your handful of soil feels dry and falls apart, it's too dry to work.

Upper right: If the soil sticks together in a clump, it's too wet to work.

Lower right: If the soil looks like this, it's just right, so get to work.

Some gardeners opt to bring in new soil instead of building their own. If you go this route, work with a reputable top-soil vendor to ensure you end up with something better than you started with. Ask friends and relatives for recommendations. Then work with the company to select the mix best suited to your needs. Many gardeners are convinced they need "black soil." The fact that it's black tells you nothing about the drainage and character of the topsoil.

Time the drainage of a 1-foot by 1-foot hole to check on the water-holding capacity of your soil.

There is a wide range of soil additives available—make sure you know what your soil really needs before you start amending it.

Ask about the screening, the composition of the mixture and the weed-seed content. Some gardening experts choose to amend the existing soil rather than bring in some unknown material.

This is also the time to address pH problems. The pH measurement tells you whether your soil is acid, often called "sour," or alkaline, referred to as "sweet." Most plants prefer a slightly acid to neutral pH of 6.0 to 7.0.

HOW MUCH IS ENOUGH

One bag of peat moss seems like a lot until you open the bag, spread the contents over the garden, and start digging. Then it vanishes quickly. Use this chart as a guide to help you order the right amount of topsoil, amendments, and mulch for your garden.

	Approximate area that can be amended with or covered by:	
	1 inch	**2 inches**
Peat moss bale size		
1 cubic foot	24 square feet	12 square feet
2.2 cubic feet	50 square feet	25 square feet
3.8 cubic feet	90 square feet	45 square feet
Compost or topsoil		
40 pound bag	16 square feet	8 square feet
Shredded mulch		
2 cubic feet	24 square feet	12 square feet

Acid-loving plants growing in high pH (above 7.0) soils often suffer from iron and manganese deficiencies. Plants that prefer alkaline soils often suffer from calcium, magnesium and sulfur deficiencies if their soil is too acidic.

Never attempt to change the soil pH without a soil test. Liming the soil to raise the pH has long-term effects. An overdose can take years to correct. Adding the amount of sulfur needed to lower the pH of alkaline soils can damage or kill plants. I prefer the low input method of managing pH—I select and grow plants suited to the existing pH.

As a small space gardener you may want to push the environmental envelope and grow plants that require a bit more work. Amending one bed to make it suitable for growing acid-loving blueberries in soil that is naturally sweet is a lot more feasible than trying to amend all the soil in the yard to accommodate an acid-loving shade tree.

Clearing the Way

You may need to eliminate some grass before building the garden. There are several ways to do this. Select the strategy that matches you gardening style, schedule and philosophy.

A hand- or power-operated sod cutter will remove pieces of the lawn, roots and all. Use these to patch bare spots in other areas of the landscape. Or place them grass-side down in the compost pile to decompose. Some garden-

The best soil amendment, whatever your soil's problems, is organic matter. It helps sandy soil hold water and clay soil drain.

Fertile soil full of organic matter is also full of earth worms, whose castings are an important source of nutrients for plants.

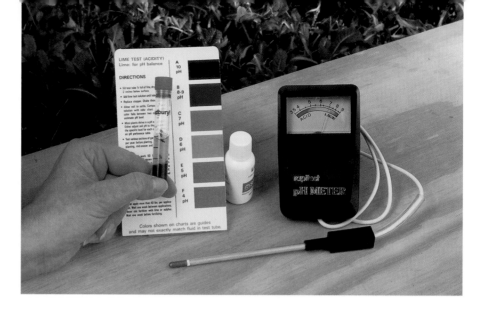

Simple kits to test soil pH are available at garden centers— make sure to follow directions carefully to get accurate results.

Lower left: **A** garden hose followed by a sprinkling of lime or outlined with landscape paint is a good way to lay out the curving edge of a new flower bed.

Lower right **S**od can be removed from the new bed using a machine or by hand, and the sod can then be used to patch the lawn elsewhere or it can be composted.

ers use these as a base for berms and other topographical changes in the landscape.

Those looking for a lower energy, non-chemical option may want to cover it up. Edge the area you're converting to a garden. Then cut the grass you want to eliminate very short, and cover it with several layers of newspaper and a few inches of woodchips, pine straw or other organic mulch.

Areas with productive, well-drained soils can be planted immediately. Push back the mulch, cut through the newspaper and sod, then plant. I found waiting a season made this process much easier. I applied the newspaper and mulch in fall and waited until spring to plant. The sod had begun to break down and the newspaper had decomposed, making planting much easier.

Wait a few months or even a season if you need to amend the soil. Cover the newspaper with shredded leaves, grass clippings or other organic matter that quickly decomposes. Once the sod has died, dig or till the dead grass layer, decomposed newspaper and mulch into the top 8 to 12 inches of soil. This kills the weeds, recycles the sod and improves the soil all in one process.

Or you can bypass the soil improvement step and cover the newspaper with 6 to 12 inches of topsoil instead of with mulch. Then you can plant immediately in your new raised bed. The sod and newspaper will not impede drainage and will eventually break down, improving the soil and allowing roots to grow into the soil below.

For quicker results or better control of perennial weeds such as quack grass and bindweed, you may want to use a total vegetation killer. Edge the area you're converting to garden, disconnecting the grass and weeds from the surrounding lawn. Spray the grass with a total vegetation killer such as Roundup® or Finale®. These products can kill anything green they touch, so apply carefully. Spray in a pattern that lets you walk only on untreated grass. I have seen footsteps of dead grass and groundcovers from gardeners walking through treated areas onto nearby plantings.

Wait the required period between chemical treatment and cultivation. You may want to make a second treatment if your yard is filled with quack grass, bindweed or annual weed seeds. Wait a few weeks after the first treatment, and if new weeds appear treat again. Some gardeners prefer to treat, amend the soil and wait for

Handle the tree roots with care. Cut any damaged roots for quicker recovery and do not bury tree roots with additional soil.

PERMEABLE PAVERS

Paved surfaces, even in a small space, can increase water runoff. Select a permeable surface to ease water problems near your home and reduce runoff into storm sewers. Select one of the new concrete materials with the "fine" left out of the mix. These materials allow water to flow through. Or use an open grid system, filling the spaces with stone or plants. Or leave space between the pavers for the water to penetrate and drain through the soil instead of running off into the street.

Rather than digging among your tree roots and risking damage to the tree, try setting pots of shade-loving plants on flagstones for a striking, artistic look.

weeds to appear. Then they make a second application after the new weed seeds or old perennial weeds reappear as a result of the tilling process.

Don't Kill the Forest or the Trees

As you improve the soil and build new gardens, be careful not to destroy the existing shade. Those age-old beauties providing shade for your garden don't like their roots disturbed. As little as an inch of soil piled on top of their roots can kill some trees. Deep cultivation destroys many of the fine feeder roots found in the top 12 to 18 inches of soil, causing trees to decline over time.

You can have your shade and flowers too. Shallow cultivation and pocket planting of perennials will help you get a permanent groundcover established beneath the trees. Use porous pavers when adding hard surfaces over the roots. I prefer steppers instead of paved pathways. The space between the steppers allows air and water to reach the roots—and of course it gives you more room to plant.

Add color and seasonal interest to these spaces by setting pots of colorful annuals in among the groundcover. You might be surprised to see how elevating a pot adds a new dimension to a garden. One botanical garden grew large-leafed hostas in big terra cotta pots beneath a stately old shade tree. The pots were set on flat stones and created quite an artistic garden scene. The hostas would have been fine planted under the tree, but this treatment was breathtaking. Check elevated planters, like other containers, daily for water needs, and fertilize as required throughout the season. Northern gardeners will need to provide special winter protection for perennials growing in pots (see chapter 4).

Dig in the Nutrients

The foundation of your garden—improved soil—is in place, and you are almost ready to start planting. Check your soil test results for recommendations on the type and amount of fertilizer your garden needs. Wait until just prior to planting to incorporate synthetic fertilizer. You want the plants in place as the fertilizer is released into the soil so it is used by the plants and not washed through to the groundwater.

Err on the conservative side if soil test recommendations are not available. Most plants don't need as much fertilizer as we think, and we don't want our plants to quickly outgrow our small space.

Consider using a slow-release, low nitrogen fertilizer. Organic materials, coated or encapsulated fertilizers, or water insoluble products release small amounts of nutrients over a longer period of time. This low level of constant feeding encourages more even growth with less risk of fertilizer burn and of poor flowering due to over-fertilization.

Consult with your local municipality or extension service for local fertilization restrictions. Due to years of over-fertilization and to groundwater and lake concerns, many communities are limiting or restricting the use of fertilizers containing phosphorus.

There are lots of options available when it comes to fertilizer, but the slow-release types that are low in nitrogen are easy for gardeners to use with minimal risk of fertilizer burn.

IT'S IN THE NUMBERS

All you need to know about a fertilizer is on the bag. You just need to do a bit of careful reading to find the information you need. Start with the three numbers in large print on the front of the bag. These represent the nutrients in the fertilizer. The first number on the left is the percent nitrogen. This nutrient is used by the plant to grow leaves, stems and all things green. It is used in the largest amounts but too much of it is not good. Excess nitrogen can injure or even kill a plant, discourage flowering and damage the environment when the excess leaches through the soil and into our ground water. Save your money and the environment by using only what the plants need.

The second or middle number represents the amount of phosphorus in the fertilizer. This nutrient encourages root development, flowering and fruiting. Blossom boosters contain high percentages of this material. Plants use phosphorus in smaller amounts than nitrogen. Years of applying balanced fertilizers such as 10-10-10 have resulted in phosphorus build-up in the soil. Many landscape soils contain high to excess amounts of this nutrient. Adding more phosphorus to these soils can interfere with the uptake of other nutrients and pollute our lakes and groundwater. This is why many communities are limiting or banning the use of fertilizers containing phosphorus.

The last number tells us how much potassium (potash) the fertilizer contains. It helps protect plants from disease, cold, drought and other stresses. A small amount compared to nitrogen is needed by the plants to gain these benefits. You often see high percentages of this nutrient in winterizing fertilizers. As with phosphorus, years of using balanced fertilizers has generally applied more potassium than needed, resulting in excess amounts in the soil. Don't add more if it is not needed.

Top-dressing your perennials with an inch or two of compost every other year is the best way to fertilize them.

Annuals generally need 1 to 3 pounds per 100 square feet of a low-nitrogen fertilizer per season. You can incorporate all 3 pounds prior to planting if you use a slow-release formulation. Otherwise make several applications throughout the season. Check the fertilizer label for recommendations.

Perennial flowers and groundcovers need even less fertilizer than annuals. Proper soil preparation and top-dressing the soil with an inch or two of compost every other year will provide most, if not all, the needed nutrients. Let the plants be your guide. Flourishing plants are a good indication the plants are getting the nutrients they need.

Wait a year after planting before fertilizing trees and shrubs. Researchers found the best results come with patience. Fertilize, if needed, in spring before growth begins or in fall after the plants are dormant. Properly watered and mulched trees and shrubs need very little fertilizer to grow and flourish.

CALCULATING QUANTITIES

Avoid buying too many plants or running short of groundcover for a bed by doing a bit of math before driving to the garden center. Now don't panic, this is basic stuff, and there's a cheat sheet below to make it easy.

Measure the length and width of each planting area. Multiply these numbers to get the square footage of the bed. Record this in your garden journal or on your landscape plan for future reference.

Next review your garden plan. Estimate or calculate the area each grouping or drift of plants will cover. Skip this step if you are filling the bed with all one variety of flower, groundcover or shrub.

Use the chart below to help calculate the number of plants needed. Consult the tag, the internet or your favorite gardening book for the recommended spacing.

Now multiply the square footage of the planting area times the number of plants per square foot. Let's use miniature impatiens as an example. Suppose I am planting them 6 inches apart in 6 square feet of garden. I would multiple 4 (plants needed per square foot) times 6 (square feet of planting space) to find that I need 24 impatiens to fill that space.

Plant Spacing (inches)	Number of Plants per Square Foot
6	4.0
8	2.25
9	1.77
10	1.44
12	1.0
15	0.64
18	0.45
24	0.25
36	0.11

Picking Up the Plants

For many of us, the most fun part of gardening is selecting and buying plants. We have our soil prepared, our design in hand and our list of plants to buy. It is off to the garden centers and nurseries to scour the aisles and racks for the perfect specimens. These are the building materials that will define, accent and beautify our outdoor living space.

Start the journey with a list of plants and the quantity of each that you need. Treat the experience as if you were grocery shopping. Go to the store on a full stomach (your completed design) and a list so you buy only those items you need. And if you stray from the list, and we all do, you'll stray less often thanks to your planning. If you lack will power, you may need a second list of friends and relatives who can use all those extra plants that won't fit into your small space!

Select and purchase only healthy plants. You do not have the space to coddle sick or struggling plants. Buy only those plants with full-sized, properly colored leaves that are free from insects and disease. Browned, spotted or tattered leaves are good clues the plant is suffering from moisture stress, disease or insect problems.

Health, not size, is the key to success in choosing plants. Smaller plants are easier to transport and manage, so the plants and your body usually survive transporting and planting unscathed. Larger plants can take longer to recover from transplanting and adapt to their new location. And larger plants also require you to dig larger holes.

Some trees and shrubs come balled and burlapped. They are dug in early spring before growth begins or in fall after the leaves drop. The trees are dug with a small portion of the rootball intact. They are usually more expensive and heavier but have a greater rate of survival than bare-root trees.

Container-grown trees, shrubs and perennials are planted and grown in pots. The smaller root systems and the pots make them easier to manage. They are moderately priced and can be planted spring through fall. Avoid heat stress on the transplants and the gardener by planting in the cooler parts of the growing season. The plants will have time to establish roots before the heat of summer.

Some shrubs, lots of roses, and some perennials are potted in spring for sale in the garden center. These potted plants were either bare-root or dug from the field and placed in containers, then grown for several months

Health, not size, is the key to success in choosing plants.

before being sold at the garden center. They may have a limited root system, which means you will need to give them special care during transplanting.

Purchase trees with straight trunks, a strong central leader (main stem) or the appropriate growth habit for that type of tree. Look for shrubs and vines with multiple stems free of damage. Annual flowers should have stout stems covered with leaves. Avoid buying leggy plants with long stems and lots of space between the leaves. Leggy plants result from overcrowding, from being too long in the flat, or from growing in too much shade. You will spend more energy grooming them back into shape than you will need to spend on keeping a healthy plant looking good. Plants that aren't yet blooming are the best, though most gardeners can't resist the beautiful blossoms. Transplants that haven't begun to bloom will focus their energy on forming roots, which means a strong root system, fuller plant and more blossoms in the long run.

Transporting Plants Safely

Clear out the trunk, backseat or trailer when you go plant shopping. Throw a tarp, a drop cloth, or other material on the floor of your transport to keep plants and the soil contained. One of my former students uses an old child's swimming pool to bring her plants home. The pool easily slides in and out of the back of her station wagon. She can fill it with flats of annuals and pots of perennials, and the sides keep the plants and soil in place on the ride home.

Fortunately most garden centers have plastic for covering car seats and carpeting. Just ask. This comes in handy when you make an unplanned stop or purchase. Keeping the seats clean for passengers often lessens the complaints about buying so many plants.

Large shrubs and trees will need a bit more room and extra care when transporting them home. Use a pickup truck, a trailer or a large vehicle to move these bigger plants. The extra space will make loading and unloading easier on you and less damaging to the plants. Loosely tie the branches to minimize breakage.

Cover the plant canopy with plastic or fabric if the leaves have started to grow and will be exposed to wind on the ride home. I cringe when I see a tree in full leaf standing straight and tall in the back of a pick-up truck. The leaves whip around in the wind as the driver concentrates on getting the new purchase home. And boy are the owners surprised, with no clue they were part of the problem, when they arrive home to find tattered leaves or when they notice, days later, that the tender leaves have browned.

Hardening off plants requires more work and more space than I have. Instead, I use floating row covers such as ReeMay®, Harvest Guard or Grass-Fast to help me harden off my tender plants. Row covers work better than a cold frame since no ventilation or construction is needed. Simply place the fabric over the plants and anchor it in place. I usually tuck the edges under the flats, or find a stray board or pipe to hold the fabric in place. The cover allows air, light and water to reach the plants while keeping them warm and protected from frost. After two weeks, if the danger of frost has passed, the plants are ready to move to their permanent locations.

Try this in your garden or on the balcony. The extra protection allows you to plant earlier and prolong the season by protecting plants from frost. Remove the row covers once the plants have adjusted and the danger of frost has passed. Simply shake off any plant debris, fold and store intact row covers in the garage for their next use.

Carefully lay large trees and shrubs on their sides. Wrap the trunk and stems with carpet or fabric anywhere they come in contact with the vehicle to prevent damage. Tie the tree in place, and don't forget the red flag for trees that extend 3 feet beyond the vehicle. Many nurseries will help with loading.

Sound like a lot of work? You may want to spend a little extra money to have the experts deliver your tree. They have the staff and equipment to handle and move large trees. Many nurseries will even place the tree in a pre-dug planting hole for you. Consider the delivery charge as an insurance policy on your initial investment.

Store newly purchased plants in a cool, shaded location until they can be planted. Cover the roots of bare-root and balled-and-burlapped trees with woodchips. Water all planting stock often enough to keep the roots moist.

Installing the Ceilings and Walls

Trees provide the living ceiling and shrubs the living walls for your garden. Plant these first whenever possible to create the framework that determines where you place other plants. Think of the process like building an addition to your home. You want the walls in place before moving in the furniture and accessories.

Just as the walls and ceilings are the mainstays of any home, trees and shrubs are the consistent long-lasting features of the landscape. Their longevity in your garden starts with proper planting.

Take one last look at the location of overhead and underground utilities. Make any last minute adjustments to your garden design and planned planting locations to avoid conflict now or when the plants reach their mature size.

Let's start with planting trees. You probably spent some significant time selecting the one or two, if you are lucky, trees for your garden hide-away. It took me a year to decide on the one tree for my little space. I wanted to be sure I received the biggest impact for the space that one tree occupied. Plant your trees properly so they will grow into the healthy beautiful specimens you desire.

PLANT TREES
WITH CARE

Avoid using tree trunks as handles or levers when moving and positioning the plants. Moving the trunk independent of the root ball damages the roots, jeopardizing your tree's health. Instead, lift and carry trees, shrubs and other plants by the container or rootball. A second set of hands will give you the strength and leverage needed to safely move large plants in the landscape.

Locate the root flare, the area where the roots flare away from the trunk, on the tree. It is often covered with soil. Untie the burlap from around the trunk of balled-and-burlapped trees. Gently brush the soil away from the trunk of the tree if the root flare is not obvious. Measure the distance from the root flare to the bottom of the rootball or container. This is equal to the depth of your planting hole.

Dig a saucer-shaped hole the same depth as the rootball (root flare to bottom) and at least two to three times wider than the root system. Avoid digging deeper than the root ball. The loosened soil is subject to settling, and soon your properly planted tree will be in a low spot that collects water and leads to root rot.

Make the hole wider than the rootball to help get the roots established. Loosening the soil in a wide area around the planting hole allows the roots to penetrate the surrounding soil for faster development of a large root system. Scratch the sides of the planting hole with your shovel. Roughening the sides eliminates glazed surfaces that are difficult for roots to penetrate.

Now the trick is to get the tree safely in the hole. Enlist a friend to help with heavier plants. Set your balled-and-burlapped tree in the hole. Double check the depth, making sure the root flare will be at or slightly above the soil surface.

Dig the hole at least twice as wide as the rootball so the tree's roots will have loose soil to grow into—loosen the roots on the side of the ball to encourage them to begin growing.

PLANTING FOR IMPACT

Maximize the impact of your plants without overstuffing your outdoor living space. Stagger the plants and rows within each grouping to maximize the view of each plant and give the appearance of a full garden. Those who don't mind a bit of extra work may want to decrease the spacing between perennials plants. Be prepared, however, to break out the shovel and start dividing them sooner than normal. But these extra divisions will give you plants to trade or win you favor from your gardening friends.

Adjust the tree so its best side is showing and its less-than-attractive side faces the fence, wall or your not-so-nice neighbor.

Remove the twine and cut away the burlap and wire cage. These materials don't decompose in most soils and can interfere with root growth and eventually girdle (strangle) the tree. Fill the planting hole with existing soil. Do not amend the soil in the planting hole with organic matter or other materials. Highly-amended soils discourage roots from moving into the less-than-ideal surrounding soil. The roots stay within the amended planting hole, never venturing beyond to form an extensive healthy root system. Gently tamp the rootball to help settle the soil and remove any air pockets.

Follow these same basic techniques when planting trees grown in containers. Roll the pot on its side or push on the container sides to loosen the roots. Some people slide the tree out of the pot and then place it in the hole. I prefer to cut off the bottom of the container and set the tree in the planting hole. Make sure the root flare is at or slightly above the soil surface and position the tree to its best vantage point.

Slice lengthwise through the side of the container and peel it away. Loosen the roots with your hands or slice through those encircling the rootball. Fill the planting hole with the existing soil.

Shrubs and vines are handled in the same manner. Check the planting location one more time to make sure there is no immediate or future conflict with utilities, your home or other structures. Plant shrubs and vines at the same depth they were growing at the nursery or in their container.

CALLING IN A PRO

Trees are a long term investment whether in a small space garden or a large landscape. Get the best value with proper care. Consult the International Society of Arboriculture's website for tips on tree planting and care. They also have a list of certified arborist for hire. These individuals passed a test and continue their education to obtain and maintain this voluntary certification. Consult one of these tree care professionals for reliable tree care advice.

Potted plants are those bare-root or field-grown plants recently potted and grown for a short time in a container. They need special care since their root systems may not be well established in the pot. Minimize the risk of damaging the roots by using this technique: cut off the bottom of the pot and place it in the planting hole, then slice the pot lengthwise and peel it away.

Mulch the soil around the new plants with a 2 to 3 inch layer of woodchips or shredded bark. Keep the chips away from the trunk and stems to avoid disease problems. Water the planting hole and surrounding soil thoroughly after planting and frequently enough over the next few weeks to keep the top 12 inches of soil moist but not wet.

Adjust your watering technique for container-grown plants. Many of these are grown in soilless mixes that dry out faster than your garden soil. Check their roots several times a week, and water often enough to keep the roots moist but not wet. Also check the surrounding soil, and water often enough to keep it moist but not wet. This may be twice a week in well-drained soils or once every ten days in cooler climates with heavy soil.

Remove any tags and broken or damaged branches from your new plants, but wait a year or two for major pruning. The more branches left on the plant, the more leaves that will be formed and the more energy produced for the plant to grow below and above ground.

Wait a year to fertilize new plantings. Fertilizer can damage the tender young roots and interfere with their establishment. Water and mulch are the best additives for establishing and growing beautiful, healthy plants.

Planting the Accessories and Floor

Now let's look at accessories and floor covering, namely flowers and groundcovers. Though some may be short-term additions to your outdoor living space, they also benefit from proper planting. Getting these plants off to a healthy start will result in better bloom, fewer pests and less maintenance for you.

Perennial flowers and groundcovers can be purchased as bare root or in 4-inch, 1-gallon or 2-gallon containers. Use larger plants if you want instant impact and smaller ones if you enjoy watching plants grow and develop. In either case leave plenty of room.

Wait a year to fertilize new tree and shrub plantings.

CAN'T MISS TIP:

HIDE THE HOSE

Keep your garden hose handy and out of sight. Hide coiled hoses in a large decorative pot. Or mount a hose caddy to the fence or wall behind a shrub or large ornamental grass. Keeping the hose handy makes it easier to water when needed. And we all know the easier the task, the more likely we are to do the job.

Perennials and other plants that arrive bare-root and still dormant should be planted immediately to prevent the roots from drying out and the plant dying.

Pot-grown perennials and annuals may have outgrown their space, sending roots out the drainage holes—remove these roots before trying to get the plant out of the pot.

Plant bare-root perennials as soon as they arrive via the mail or are purchased from the store. If the weather is bad, store the plants in a cool location, such as a root cellar or refrigerator, until they can be planted outdoors. Keep the packing material around the roots moist. Sometimes the plants start to grow in transit or on the shelf of the garden center. Pot up any of the bare-root plants that have begun growing. Keep them in a cool bright location free from frost, and gradually introduce them to the outdoors.

Perennials in containers may cost a bit more, but I find them easier to manage with my busy schedule and low maintenance garden philosophy. I can buy plants when I have time to shop, then store them in a cool shaded area, water as needed, and plant as my schedule allows. Plus I have a longer planting season to get them into the ground. And if I run out of time, I can sink the pot in a vacant spot in the garden until next season when more time or space may be available.

Water the plants the night before you plan to put them in the garden. Moistening the rootball helps the plant deal with the transplanting process. Carefully remove container-gown perennials from the pot when you're ready to plant. Push on the sides of the pot or roll large containers on the ground. Then slide the plant out, don't pull on the stems. Loosen pot-bound roots, or use a sharp knife or hand pruners to slice through the rootball in several places. This encourages roots to grow into the surrounding soil.

Use a trowel or shovel to dig a hole the same depth but twice as wide as the plant's rootball. Set the plant in the hole and backfill with the existing soil. Make sure the crown of the plant—the point at which the roots meet the stem—is at or just slightly below the soil surface. Avoid both shallow planting that causes plants to dry out and deep planting that leads to crown rot and plant death. Gently tamp the soil, and water the plant to help eliminate air pockets and settle the soil.

Annuals are colorful accessories that provide quick impact in any size garden. Their long-lasting blooms and colorful flowers can brighten, unify, add pizzazz, or give a sense of serenity to any space.

Timing is critical to growing beautiful annuals. Planting warm-weather annuals in cool soil delays their growth and flowering. Planting cool-weather annuals in the heat of summer prevents bloom and plant development. But waiting for the right time to plant is easier said than done. I find patience

Left: **S**queeze the sides of the pot gently to loosen the rootball before removing the plant from the pot.

Right: **T**hese healthy roots need a little loosening to ensure they extend into the soil—gently pull some of the bottom and side roots out from the rootball.

After the plant is in the ground, water it carefully to settle the soil and remove any air pockets.

This healthy hollyhock transplant is well on the way to putting out new growth in its new home.

the most difficult gardening skill for most of us to master.

Slowly harden off plants for their move outdoors while you are waiting for the proper planting time. Annuals started indoors or those moving directly from the greenhouse to the outdoors need help adjusting to their new environment. Gradually expose them to the cool temperatures and direct sunlight outside. After two weeks they will be ready for their permanent outdoor location. Use this waiting period to prepare your soil if you have not already done so.

Water these transplants, like your perennials, the night before planting. Check planting tags for specific information on spacing and care.

Set the plants out in the area you will be planting. Arrange them on the soil surface to make planting easier and quicker. Adjust the spacing and arrangement as needed and then dig in.

Carefully remove the transplants from their containers. Squeeze the planting pack and slide out the transplant. Gently massage the roots of pot-bound plants to encourage the roots to grow beyond the rootball and into the surrounding soil. One landscaper friend calls this "teasing" the roots. I always picture the gardeners taunting the plants as they put them in the garden.

Use a trowel to dig a hole larger than the plant's rootball. Set the plant in the hole at the same depth it was growing in the container. Cover the roots with soil, gently tamp, and water. Watch for settling and cover exposed roots with soil if needed.

Remove the flowers and pinch back leggy transplants. This encourages root development and branching for fuller plants. If you can't stand to sacrifice the flowers for the roots, try removing the flowers on every other plant or in every other row. Remove the remaining flowers as the other plants start to form new blooms

Have a lightweight blanket, row cover or other frost protection handy. Be prepared to cover early plantings if an unexpected frost moves into the area. I keep these materials on hand in the fall as well. Protecting the plants from the first couple frosts in fall often allows me to enjoy the garden several weeks longer until the weather makes a more permanent turn for the cold.

Don't forget to put a few bulbs in the garden, including plants that grow from rhizomes (iris and cannas), corms (crocus and gladiolus), tubers (dahlias), and other underground structures that are generally grouped with true bulbs such as tulips and daffodils. These plants can add color to groundcovers, extend the bloom in a perennial display, or supplement the beauty of annuals.

Plant spring-flowering bulbs like tulips and daffodils, as well as summer-blooming lilies and alliums, in the fall. These bulbs need a period of cold temperatures to bloom. Plant bulbs two to three times as deep as their height. Arrange and properly space the bulbs on the soil surface. Use a bulb planter or trowel to set bulbs at the proper depth and spacing.

Bulbs treated like perennials need to stay in place with their leaves intact for at least six to eight weeks after flowering. Try mixing the bulbs with perennials, annuals or other plantings to help mask the declining foliage. I like to use pansies as a groundcover for my bulbs, or scatter minor bulbs like crocus among my summer-blooming perennials and autumn crocus throughout my groundcover for added bloom.

Less hardy spring and summer bloomers like calla lilies, gladiolus, dahlias, cannas and elephant ears need different care. Purchase bulbs to start indoors for earlier bloom outdoors, or plant the bulbs directly outdoors after the soil has warmed. Most of these plants won't tolerate any frost, so harden off transplants and wait to move them into the garden until after the last spring frost. Consult the tags for specific directions on planting and season-long care.

Don't forget to put a few bulbs in the garden.

MEASURE FIRST, THEN WATER

Invest in a rain gauge to help monitor rainfall in your garden. There are simple ones you can camouflage in the garden or attractive ones that look like a piece of art to be admired. Place the rain gauge in an area free from obstruction so you will get an accurate reading of the rain falling in your garden. Use this information to help determine timing and amount of water needed.

Dig these plants up in fall after a light freeze has killed the tops. Allow the bulbs to dry, gently clean off excess soil, pack in peat moss or sand, and store in a cool dark location. Some of these summer-flowering plants like cannas (hardy zones 8) can be treated like perennials and left outdoors in southern gardens.

If all this seems like too much work, consider treating these non-hardy bulbs as annuals. You may only need a couple to color up your small space garden making this an affordable option.

Post-Planting Care

Once in the ground your plants need your help to settle in and thrive in their new location. Water the transplants, thoroughly moistening the top 6 inches of soil. Check new plantings several times a week. Water whenever the top few inches of soil are moist and crumbly. Gradually extend the time between waterings. This helps encourage deep roots that are more tolerant of drought.

Left: After frost, dig up dahlia bulbs, clean them off, dry them, then store them for the winter in containers of peat moss or sand.

Right: Watering chores can be reduced by use of an irrigation system and a rain gauge to measure rainfall and determine how much additional water is needed.

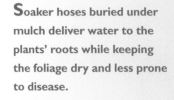

Once established, flowering plants will need to be watered less frequently. So how often should you water? It depends on the soil, air temperature, humidity and type of plant you are growing. I like to let my plants and the soil they are growing in guide me. Unfortunately our plants won't order up a drink of water, but they do provide subtle and not so subtle clues when we need to give them a drink. Watch the plants for a slight change of leaf color (from bright to dull or gray green) or decrease in firmness. Don't wait too long. Drought-stressed plants are more susceptible to pests, and they're short lived and unsightly. We can't waste precious space on ugly plants.

Check the soil during dry periods. Most plants prefer moist, well-drained soils and an inch of water a week. Water whenever the top few inches of soil are crumbly and moist. Supplement rainfall when needed with a thorough soaking once a week in clay soil and twice a week in sandy soil. Water plants less often in cooler or humid weather and more frequently in hot and dry conditions. Allow the soil to become drier before watering drought-tolerant annuals, perennials, cacti and succulents.

Water early in the day to reduce the risk of disease and the amount of water lost to evaporation. Consider using a watering wand, soaker hose, or drip-irrigation system to keep the water off the plants and on the soil where it is needed.

Even small space gardeners are turning to irrigation systems to reduce time spent watering. These systems allow you to apply water when needed and at the right time. Properly designed systems used correctly can actually reduce water wasted through improper watering.

Soaker hoses buried under mulch deliver water to the plants' roots while keeping the foliage dry and less prone to disease.

Watering by hand is time-consuming, but it's a good way to spend quality time inspecting the health of your plants.

WATERING TIPS

Planting a water-wise garden is good for the environment and easier for you to maintain.

- **Select plants adapted to your climate.** Plants that thrive with the average amount of rainfall in your area will need less supplemental watering once established. Check them during extended periods of drought as they may need a helping hand.

- **Group plants by watering needs.** You can design and program your irrigation system to match plants' needs. If you have a manual system—you—it will be quicker and easier to manage the plants.

- **Plant moisture-loving plants near the water source.** A shorter hose or quicker trip with the sprinkling can is all that will be needed to get water to these plants.

- **Collect water in rain barrels for use in the garden.** New designs make them easier to use and incorporate into small spaces.

Many of the insects in your garden are helpful—the praying mantis is a predator that loves chowing down on harmful leaf-eaters such as aphids, flies, and grasshoppers.

Conserve moisture and reduce the need to water by mulching the soil. Cover the soil surface with a thin layer of shredded leaves, cocoa bean shells, pine straw or other organic material. Here's a trick to speed up the process and avoid burying the plants with mulch. Cover new transplants with an empty pot after planting and just prior to mulching. Fork the mulch onto the bed and spread over the soil surface and around the pots. Lift the pots when the mulching is complete.

Mulches conserve moisture so you need to water less often. I prefer organic mulches that break down and add organic matter and nutrients to the soil. Limit mulch around plants that need well-drained soils and suffer root and crown rot in damp soils.

Mulching is one of those garden tasks that provides double, even quadruple, the benefits for your effort. Use mulch to control weeds, protect soil, and moderate soil temperatures. A blanket of mulch over the soil surface blocks the sunlight, limiting weed-seed germination. This means fewer weeds for you to pull.

CAN'T MISS TIP:

COCOA BEAN MULCH

Just the smell of chocolate can tempt us and our dogs. This confectionary delight is bad for our waistlines, but it's deadly to our dogs. Avoid cocoa bean shell mulch if you own a dog. The smell and flavor have tempted many a dog to eat the mulch. Some survive, others get sick, and some vets have reported finding a gut full of cocoa bean mulch in the dog's stomach during an autopsy.

Mulch the soil to protect it from compaction and erosion caused by heavy rains pounding directly on the soil. Organic mulches help keep soils cooler in the summer and warmer at night.

Keep Them Growing

All your tender loving care will produce lots of plants, including weeds, growing in your garden. Your healthy plants will be able to compete with most of these unwanted guests, but you will probably need to lend a helping hand. Mulching eliminates many weeds before they start growing. The few annual weeds that sprout through the mulch are relatively easy to pull. Since small gardens usually are packed full of plants, it's seldom wise to hoe the weeds out—you may find you get rid of more desirable plants than you do weeds.

If you decide to go the chemical route, read and follow all label directions carefully before using herbicides (weed killers). These are plant killers that don't know the difference between a petunia and a dandelion. Spot-treat weeds with the right chemical to minimize the negative impact on the environment. Or try some of the newer, more environmentally friendly products on the market. Corn gluten works as pre-emergent weed control, and soap- or vinegar-derived products burn off the tops of existing weeds. These are gentler on the environment, but you may have to settle for less than perfect control while making repeat applications.

Pests and Diseases

Other unwelcome guests include insects and diseases. These can ruin our plants' appearance, slow their growth, injure and even kill them. The best defense against pests is a healthy plant. You started in that direction by properly preparing the soil, doing your planting right and providing the correct amounts of water and mulch.

Selecting pest-resistant cultivars and starting with pest-free plants also reduce future problems. Monitor your plants throughout the season, watching for signs of unwelcome guests. Only about 3 percent of all the insects in your garden are harmful, but when I discover some that are, I like to pick them off and squash them. If this makes you squeamish, try blasting them off the plants with a strong blast of water.

Large destructive pest populations may need a bit more intervention. Yellow dishes filled with soapy water can help attract and kill aphids and other

While these caterpillars will do lots of snacking on any fennel you have in the garden, they'll repay you with their beauty when they turn into swallowtail butterflies.

harmful insects. Shallow dishes of stale beer will attract slugs and snails. As they crawl inside for a drink, they drown. What a way to go!

Or try some of the newer, more environmentally friendly products. Soaps, plant-based oils, neem and other products have been developed to control insects while being gentle on the plants and the environment. Read and follow all the label directions for best results.

Diseases can often be controlled with a little good housekeeping. Remove infected plant parts as soon as the disease appears. Remove and destroy insect- and disease-infested plants at the end of the season. Do not compost, as most of our compost piles do not heat up enough to kill these pests and diseases.

If additional control is needed, start with more environmentally friendly control options. Cornell University found 1 tablespoon of baking soda mixed with 1 teaspoon of horticulture (lightweight or summer) oil in a gallon of water controlled powdery mildew. Start applying the mix at the first sign of the disease and continue weekly throughout the season.

Or try some of the other environmentally friendly disease-fighters such as copper (long used by organic gardeners), plant-based fungicides and neem. Get the best results and avoid problems by reading and following label directions whenever using any product, whether organic or synthetic.

Some unwelcome guests may be a bit larger. Animals can wreak havoc in any size garden. Fences help keep many critters out of the garden. Add a barrier between the ground and bottom edge of the fence to keep out small animals such as voles and baby rabbits. Sink the barrier into the ground to discourage animals that like to dig.

Japanese beetles are among the most destructive of pests, decimating roses and other plants during their six weeks above ground. Some gardeners hand-pick them and drop them into containers of alcohol.

Holes in your hosta leaves almost certainly mean slugs, which can be controlled with a variety of home remedies, such as saucers of beer.

Homemade and commercial repellents may provide some relief. Apply them before the animals start dining. It is easier to prevent feeding rather than it is to break a bad habit. Vary the repellents you use to increase the chance of success.

Scare tactics such as rubber snakes and plastic owls, clanging pans and whirligigs may help. Move them around so the animals don't become accustomed to their presence. Use a variety of strategies to help minimize animal damage.

Grooming

Keep plants looking good with a bit of ongoing care. A pinch here and a clip there keep stray branches out of pathways and flowers in bloom.

Remove faded flowers on annuals and perennials to encourage continual bloom. This allows the plants to put their energy into producing new flowers rather than setting seed. Cut back the faded flower to the first set of healthy leaves. You may see the second set of flowers already starting to form. Continue throughout the season to keep annuals in full bloom. You may want to leave the last flush of flowers on perennials and roses allowing seedpods and rose hips to form. These add beauty and help attract birds to the winter garden.

Some plants such as impatiens and catmint need little or no deadheading to look good all season. Look for plants labeled as free-flowering or self-cleaning. These plants shed old flowers making room for new blooms. If you don't like the fallen petals of impatiens on the patio, keep these and other self-cleaning plants toward the inside of the garden where the falling flowers won't annoy you if you are a meticulous gardener.

Cut back leggy or floppy annuals to encourage more compact growth and continuous bloom. Use hand pruners or garden scissors to cut the stems back halfway. Prune above a set of healthy leaves and wait for new growth and flowers to appear.

Prune perennials to control plant height, reduce floppiness, and delay flowering. Cut back late-summer and fall-blooming perennials like sedum, coneflower, asters, and mums early in the season. This encourages shorter stiffer branches that won't need staking. Stop pruning by late June in the north and mid-July in the south to avoid interfering with bloom.

Get creative and use pruning to grow your own plant stakes and extend the bloom time. Pinch only the outer ring of stems on coneflowers, Shasta daisies, and other tall perennials. The center stems will grow taller and

Removing faded flowers from peonies—deadheading—keeps the plant looking tidy the rest of the season.

Pinching back fall-blooming perennials such as chrysanthemums early in the season keeps the plants from getting out of bounds and floppy before they bloom.

The faded blossoms of daylilies can be broken off by hand to keep the plants looking tidy as bloom continues.

Cutting flowers in the garden provides an added way to prune—be careful not to cut off buds developing lower on the plant.

bloom earlier. The outer stems will be shorter and stiffer, supporting the center, and bloom later.

You may need to give tall annuals and perennials a little added help in standing straight. Mix in a few sturdy neighbors such as ornamental grass or small shrubs to provide support and keep floppy plants in check. Or use the old English technique of placing twigs in among the plants. Branches pruned from hedges are strategically placed in and around the plants. As the plants grow, they cover the support, often camouflaging it from view.

Grow-through stakes and cages that allow floppy plants to grow up through the support are widely available for purchase. You still get some plant movement and much of the structure is masked by the plant. Make a note in your garden journal or on your calendar to put stakes and cages in place as soon as the plants needing them appear. Shoving a mature plant into a cage can damage the plant and make it look as if you tried to squeeze a large plant into a small space.

Pruning

Now let's move a bit higher up in the garden and discuss pruning the vines, shrubs, and trees. No other gardening chore evokes such a wide range of emotions as pruning. Feelings range from pruning paranoia, fear of killing or maiming the plant, to visions of a chainsaw massacre. Before breaking out the tools, make sure there is a reason to prune. You should prune to maintain size, to improve flowering, fruiting, or bark color, or to remove damaged or diseased branches.

Prune spring-flowering shrubs such as lilac and forsythia in spring right after they flower. Spring-bloomers flower on the previous season's growth, so pruning in late summer or winter removes the next year's flower buds and eliminates the spring display.

Trim summer-blooming plants during the dormant season. Potentilla, hills-of-snow hydrangeas, and summer-blooming spireas flower on the current season's growth.

Prune junipers, boxwoods and other evergreen shrubs in early spring before growth begins or in mid-July when they are semi-dormant. Northern gardeners should avoid fall pruning that opens up plants to damage from winter wind and sun.

Remove dead, damaged or disease-infected branches whenever and wherever they are found. Disinfect tools with rubbing alcohol between cuts to prevent the spread of disease.

Thinning the stems of fast-spreading plants such as bee balm not only keeps the plant in bounds, it also reduces disease problems by increasing room for air circulation.

Winterizing

Northern gardeners may want to build in a little winter insurance. Mulch borderline hardy or expensive perennials, or those you planted late, in the fall after the ground freezes. Evergreen boughs, straw or marsh hay insulate the plants and soil preventing fluctuating temperatures that lead to untimely sprouting and frost-heaving.

Gardeners with reliable snow cover don't need to worry—nature has taken care of the winter mulching chores. Those with mid-winter thaws and sporadic snow cover may want to give nature a hand. Or use my approach—plants that are not hardy enough to survive winter on their own won't be in my garden next year.

Broadleaf evergreens, grafted roses and other tender plants may need extra protection the first year or even throughout their life if you pushed them beyond their hardiness zone or planted them in a less-than-desirable location. Use hardware cloth (smaller mesh and sturdier than chicken wire) to encircle the plants. Sink the hardware cloth several inches into the soil to keep out voles and other small critters. Use a 4-foot tall fence to help keep rabbits at bay. Wait for the soil to freeze, and then fill the cylinder of wire mesh with straw or evergreen boughs. This reduces winter damage caused by drying winds and sun.

Use a piece of fencing, your discarded holiday tree, or a make-shift barrier of burlap or other fabric as a windbreak. Protect newly-planted and broadleaf evergreens from winter winds that can dry the needles and leaves, causing then to brown and drop.

Remove winter mulch and other protection in spring after the severe weather has passed, temperatures begin hovering around freezing, or the plants begin to grow. Recycle the winter mulch right in the garden. Use it as a soil mulch, ingredient in the compost pile, or chip evergreen boughs to use as mulch around trees and shrubs.

If all this sounds like too much work, it really isn't. First of all, you have a small space, which means fewer plants to manage. If you prepare the site correctly and select the right plants for your growing conditions (see Chapter 5), you have eliminated most of the work. Proper planting and minimal routine maintenance will keep your plants healthy throughout the growing season and for many years to come.

Grow-through plant supports are good for large plants with heavy blooms such as peonies. Here the grid portion of the support is laid over the budding plant in early spring.

As the peony grows, the grid portion of the support is lifted and the legs are attached.

Challenges and Opportunities

as you have discovered in earlier chapters, the same principles apply whether you're designing and planting a small or a large garden. Creating an attractive and functional small space hideaway has its special opportunities and also, needless to say, its special challenges.

When I consult with homeowners who are starting to develop their large one-, two- or even ten-acre lots, I suffer a bit of jealousy tempered by a sense of satisfaction. These gardeners have boundless opportunities, wide open spaces and lots of land to develop and maintain. I envy them the expanse of land to create the gardens and spaces of their dreams. But I also appreciate how overwhelming these seemingly endless spaces can be. So maybe our small gardens aren't so bad after all!

In the meantime we have more small space opportunities to discuss. We will create some space using pots and containers, brighten up the shade, and let some sunshine in, doubling and maybe even tripling the impact of the plantings in our small garden.

Varying the height of your containers and of the plants they hold helps create an interesting composition.

Container Gardens

An easy way to add gardening space is to use containers. I have always gardened in pots. When I lived in apartments, containers were my only gardening option. They lined the entryway, filled my tiny balcony and landed any place my landlord would allow. When I finally bought my home, there still wasn't enough room for all the plants I wanted to grow.

Containers also allow me to add fragrance and beauty in areas with no in-ground planting space. Plus they give me room to try new plant introductions. When grown in a pot, only a few plants are needed, so I can try one or two and see if their performance merits precious space in my garden.

Containers can hold shrubs as well as smaller perennials and annuals—here, butterfly bush and popcorn bush mingle with more traditional container dwellers in an appealing grouping.

Take a look around your small space. Do you need to add a little living color or interest where there is no ground to plant? This was the case with my back patio, which covers the space from the wall of the garage to the back wall of my house. The patio surface is white concrete, one wall is white siding on my porch and the other is brick on my garage. All these hard surfaces make the area a bit sterile and unwelcoming.

I filled a few pots with vines to cover the walls, tropical and annuals for added color, and a couple of watermelons and squash to cover the surface while providing food and fun. I still hate the concrete surface, but the plants gave me an affordable, fast option for changing the look of my patio.

I have seen creative gardeners use pots to mask unsightly views, fill in voids or create a sanctuary amongst concrete and steel. Look for bare spaces in your outdoor living space, such as a corner where two walls meet with nothing but siding to view. Or perhaps you need to cover the air conditioning unit, the gas meter, or some other utility that not only fills valuable garden space but creates an eyesore. A container garden may be the solution.

Like the rest of your landscape, containers can provide year-round interest. Start off the season with a burst of color from tulips, daffodils or other bulbs mixed with frost-tolerant annuals. One of my favorite spring container gardens used colorful rainbow Swiss chard as a vertical accent, a few tulips and pansies for additional color, and vinca vine as a trailer.

Follow the spring display with a summer collection of flowers, grasses, edibles and tropicals. Fall can be a combination of mums, asters, ornamental kale and cabbage, and grasses. For winter, our southern friends can grow cold-tolerant plants, while those in the north may need to rely on evergreen boughs, colorful branches and other cut materials.

PLANTS FOR CONTAINER GARDENS

Think of your container garden as a miniature flower garden or floral arrangement. Color, texture, balance and unity all apply, just on a very small scale. Use a vertical accent to provide scale with the pot and surrounding environment. Trailing plants can also keep container planting in scale. Trailing vines and flowering plants help connect the plantings to the pot while softening its structure. Use medium-sized plants for filler. These plants bridge the tall and short plants, add lots of interest and showcase the focal points of the arrangement. Here are just a few examples:

Vertical Accents

- Spike, dracaena or cordyline
- Bananas, cannas, brugmansia, *Phormium*, and other tropicals
- Sunflower, *Verbena bonariensis*, and other spiky annuals
- Fountain grass, ornamental grasses, and variegated bamboo
- Russian sage, bugbane, and other perennials
- 'Purple Majesty' millet, ornamental corn
- Swiss chard, eggplant, peppers, and tomatoes
- Small-scale trees and shrubs
- Mandevilla, bougainvillea, and other vines trained on a small trellis or obelisk

Trailers

- Vinca vine—traditional but look for new varieties
- *Dichondra* 'Silver Falls', green or golden moneywort
- Variegated yellow archangel (*Lamium galeobdolon*) or dead nettle (*Lamium maculatum*)
- Licorice and sweet potato vines
- Mandevilla
- German, English or other ivies

Containers can serve a variety of design purposes—here they form a screen to provide some seclusion for a garden bench.

- Fuchsia, petunias, diascias, nasturtiums, lobelias and other trailing annuals
- Strawberry plant with runners or spider plant with offsets

Fillers

- Pansies, impatiens, pentas, strobilanthes, heliotrope, verbena and other annuals
- Baby's breath, coral bells, hosta and other perennials
- Sage, parsley, basil and other herbs
- Small peppers, patio tomatoes and eggplants
- Coleus, rex begonias, other foliage and houseplants
- Tulips, daffodils, crocus and other bulbs
- Plumbago and other small shrubs and dwarf evergreens
- Ferns, smaller grasses and sedges

WEATHERING A POT

Old is in and you can speed up the aging process on terra cotta pots with a little time and yogurt. Paint the outside of the pot with a layer of yogurt to attract algae and lichens to form. Set the pot outside for a week or so to dry before planting. Soon the pot will be covered with green just like an old weathered pot.

The other option is one a student shared. Her company buried terra cotta pots in manure over winter. In spring, they removed the pots, let them dry for a week and planted. I don't know about you, but I will opt for the yogurt.

Containers have gone to new heights in this garden—though a bit hard to water, the potted geraniums perched on recycled porch posts are certainly striking. And notice in the background that the space between tree and ground is filled beautifully by hanging baskets.

Many gardeners include small trees and shrubs in their container gardens. Just as in the landscape, these provide year-round structure, evergreen foliage, colorful bark and sometimes berries. Select plants at least one or two zones hardier than your zone to increase over-wintering success. Those in cold harsh climates or growing tender plants will need to provide extra winter care. Those in the south must select heat-tolerant plants, provide plenty of water and avoid heat-absorbing containers.

Containers also allow you to add color and interest in the void between the tree canopy and ground layer. Try filling the space with plants and see what happens. A hanging basket or two slung over the lower branch of a tree can brighten this space and help screen the view beyond. Or add a basket that echoes the colors of the bed below and see what greater impact you generate. Use a wide cloth strap over the branch to avoid damaging the tree.

An added benefit of container gardening is easy access to the plants. If bad knees, arthritis or other physical limitations are keeping you from gardening, containers may be the answer. Pots help elevate plants for easier access. Pull up a chair and you can sit down to garden. Hanging baskets, window boxes and wall-mounted containers can be placed within reach for you to tend and enjoy. Add a pulley to hanging baskets so they can be raised and lowered for easier access. This is helpful even if your comfort with lifting and reaching is not limited. How many of us have ended up with a soaked arm as we reached up to water our flower baskets!

Avoid cluttering your small space with too many baskets and containers. With a small space it doesn't take much to go overboard. Too many containers with too much variety will make your space feel even smaller. I know it is hard to resist, but we must. Like many of you, I collect plants and pots for those plants, filling every nook and cranny with a pot

or basket. It is time to let go of the clutter or avoid it before you get started. Go back to your landscape design and use the templates from page 166 to place pots within your outdoor living area. Make sure they do not block traffic flow or fill too much of your relaxing and entertaining space.

As you start creating your container garden, decide whether you want a collection of pots grouped together to create a garden or an individual pot filled with a variety of plants. Pots within the grouping don't need to be exactly the same, but they should blend together in style, color or another unifying feature.

Whether in a group or standing alone, containers are a critical part of the garden environment and overall décor. Decide whether you want the container or the plants to be the focal point of the contained garden. The plants and container must complement each other, but you may want to highlight an antique pot or work of art by selecting plants that accent the piece. In this case, the plants should echo the color and elements of the pot so it remains the focal point.

Or maybe you want to grow some interesting plant combinations or include dazzling new varieties and don't care if anyone notices the container. A simple terra cotta pot or colorful ceramic pot complements the plants, but the flowers definitely steal the show.

Some gardeners create displays where the container is virtually "non-existent." I have seen several wall mounted containers completely covered

Unity and repetition in the garden can come from containers—multiple pots climbing the stairs serve exactly that design purpose.

Planters come in a variety of sizes, shapes and materials. Look for materials that fit your gardening needs, climate and décor. Evaluate such characteristics as moisture retention, durability, rot resistance, UV resistance and ability to withstand winter.

Terra cotta pots are a traditional favorite. Many gardeners are now painting or covering them with moss for added interest. Plain terra cotta pots dry out more quickly than glazed or plastic pots. They are heavy and need to be moved indoors for cold winter storage.

Plastic pots come in a variety of styles and colors. They are generally light-weight and retain moisture better than clay. Look for UV-resistant pots, and store them indoors where winters are harsh. Rigid plastic pots become brittle and crack from exposure to sunlight, extreme heat and cold. Use semi-flexible plastic pots for over-wintering plants.

Recycled plastic pots save plastic from entering the landfill. Select those with thicker walls that make them more durable while insulating plants from hot and cold temperature extremes. They are less apt to crack and break like plastic and terra cotta. These are nonporous with good water retention.

Rubber pots made from recycled tires or a combination of recycled rubber and plastic are also good for the environment. They look like terra cotta but are lighter in weight and don't break when dropped. A variety of sizes and colors are available. These are nonporous so they have good water retention.

Wood containers are generally long lasting. Select containers made from long-lasting hardwoods or lumber treated with a plant-friendly preservative to increase their longevity. Though the wood is porous, it retains water resulting in good water retention. Purchase well-constructed planters that will stay intact as wood shrinks and swells.

Stone and concrete are long-lasting and heavy. Use these planters where weight is not a concern. They can heat up in the summer but also provide good insulation for winter. These are good choices for permanent placement since they weather well and are heavy to move.

Metal planters are generally durable and heavy. They hold moisture but heat up quickly in the sun. Stay vigilant with watering or the roots will bake and dry up.

Synthetic materials such as fiberglass and resin are generally lightweight and durable. Many look natural or classic and may even change as they age. Price and winter weather tolerance vary.

with plants. They looked more like a flower arrangement than a pot of flowers. A friend of mine designs spectacular container gardens in black plastic nursery pots—the ones shrubs arrive in. Since his focus is on new and different plants or interesting combinations, he wants nothing to detract from their beauty. The black pots are quickly covered with plants, and any bit of the pot that does show through is easily overlooked.

Container Basics

Whether you are selecting a container to serve as an accent in your garden or just as a vessel to hold soil, it must be suitable for plant growth. Select a container with drainage holes. No matter how experienced you are, it is nearly impossible to apply just the right amount of water each time you water a container. The excess collects and fills up the bottom of the pot, leading to root rot. Then nature adds an inch or two of rain and suddenly your plants are floating.

Most pots come with drainage holes; if your container doesn't, add your own. Consult an expert before drilling into that expensive piece of pottery or antique metal basket. If you must have the pot and there are no drainage holes, then try double-potting. Place a slightly smaller container with drainage holes inside the decorative pot.

CAN'T MISS TIP:

WATERING PIPE

Increase success when growing plants in strawberry pots, planting bags, and wall gardens. These containers have planting pockets from top to bottom. The water only reaches the top row or two of plants before running out the holes. Add a watering pipe down the center of the container to correct this problem. Use a piece of PVC pipe with holes drilled in the sides or a cylinder of chicken wire filled with sphagnum moss. Water through the top opening of the pipe. The water will move from the pipe to the surrounding soil ensuring all plants receive their fair share of water.

Unassuming clay pots let the plants be the stars.

DOUBLE POTTING

Double potting will help you use decorative pots that lack drainage holes. Fill the bottom of the decorative pot with stones, Styrofoam™ packing peanuts or other loose material. This reservoir will capture excess water. Now find a pot that will rest upon the filler and stay hidden inside the larger container. Fill the inside pot liner with planting mix and flowers.

Set the planted pot inside the beautiful container. Cover the soil and edge with sphagnum moss if needed to hide the mechanics. Now when you water thoroughly, the excess collects in the reservoir and the plant roots are held above it. Check weekly or after a rain storm to make sure the water hasn't risen over the stones leaving the plants sitting in water.

Empty the reservoir as needed. I simply lift the inside pot, secure the pebbles, and pour off the excess water. It's a bit messy but it works. Other gardeners use tubing to siphon out the excess water without disturbing the planting.

The spiral topiary in this container leads the eye upward along the window.

Those with limited time or who are frequently out of town may want to invest in self-watering containers. The bottom of the pot is a reservoir that holds water. The water moves from the reservoir into the planting mix by capillary action. Other systems use fabric wicks to move the water from the reservoir to the soil. Some have weep holes to prevent a buildup of water. If not, you may want to add your own to prevent root rot. Try a couple and see if they match your gardening style before investing a lot of money.

The size of the pot is important from both a design and maintenance perspective. The pot should be about 1/3 the total height of the contained garden. Larger than this, the pot can overwhelm the plants and smaller than this the plants overpower the pot.

Large pots hold more soil that can retain water longer and insulate roots better than smaller pots. This means less watering for you and better protection from heat and cold for the plant's roots. But, large pots filled with soil are heavy. This may be a concern for balcony gardeners or those who need to move planters in and out for winter or around the landscape when entertaining guests.

A variety of container styles, sizes, and materials nevertheless works well together in this patio grouping.

Select a material that complements your outdoor living space décor and planting scheme. An antique pot may be hard to blend when the landscape scheme is modern with clean lines. The color is also a consideration. A brightly colored festive pot may disrupt the serenity of a meditation garden.

MOVING PLANTS INDOORS AND OUT

Moving tropicals and houseplants in and out for summer and winter can be hard on you and the plants. Gradually introduce the plants to their new environment.

Wait until the danger of frost has passed to move plants outdoors. Gradually increase the amount of light the plant receives each day. Cover or move back indoors when temperatures drop. Check soil moisture daily and water as needed.

In fall, start moving plants back indoors as the temperatures hover in the low 50s or high 40s. Start by moving the plants to a sheltered location such as a screened porch or a vacant room isolated from your other plants. Place in the sunniest window or under artificial lights. If possible, keep the plants in a well-lit location all winter. If this is not possible, gradually over a two-week period reduce the amount of light the plant receives. Check the soil moisture and water thoroughly as needed.

Continue to check for pests. I only treat if problems arise. I prefer people- and cat-friendly products such as insecticidal soap or neem. Yellow sticky traps will help reduce white fly populations to a tolerable level. If pest problems are too bad, I may sacrifice one plant for the health of my indoor garden.

Potted Meyer lemons move indoors and out with the seasons—here, they nestle behind an edging of germander. Notice the hen and chicks planters on the stairs to the door.

The material also should be suited to your climate. Some types of pots can be used outdoors year round, while others need to move in for the winter or get too hot in the summer sun. Weight, as well as durability, may be a concern. Stone and concrete planters are long-lasting but heavy, while plastic and some of the new synthetics are light-weight. A heavy pot is less likely to blow over in the wind or topple from the weight of tall plants. Light-weight containers may be a better choice for mounting on a fence or setting on a balcony.

Choose the material that fits your maintenance schedule. Breathable materials such as terra cotta tend to dry out quickly, while glazed pots and plastic retain water, meaning less frequent watering. Metal tends to heat up and dry the soil, requiring more frequent watering.

Planting the Pot

Start with a clean pot. Use a 10 percent bleach solution to remove disease organisms and salt accumulation. Only clean the inside of pots covered with lichens, moss, or a green patina. You may be thinking, "I never clean my pots and I have never had a problem." That's great, but if a disease is lurking in the pot it can wipe out your planting. This is a loss you could have avoided with a small investment of time and energy before the season started.

Select a well-drained potting mix that retains moisture. I used to mix my own, trying new and different combinations each season. I started with the traditional $1/3$ soil, $1/3$ peat moss and $1/3$ vermiculite or perlite. I then varied the mix using equal parts of soil and compost with some vermiculite or perlite added for drainage. Occasionally, I bought a commercial potting mix and doctored it up to fit my low-maintenance gardening style. I liked using soil to help retain water and nutrients, but it got harder to find small quantities of quality topsoil, and there is always the concern about pests and weeds.

Fortunately, many of the newer container mixes have improved. I look for consistency from bag to bag and season to season. The mix also needs to hold moisture. I do not mind watering pots daily, but more often does not fit into my gardening regime.

Check out the bag to get the scoop on the product before you add it to your shopping cart. Select a sterile product with good water retention.

CONSERVING PLANTING MIX

Large pots require lots of planting mix. If weight or the price of potting mix concerns you, try a false bottom. Fill the bottom third of the container with non-degradable packing peanuts, crushed soda cans, or other light-weight draining material. Cover with weed barrier or other non-degradable fabric that will hold the soil above but allow water to drain through. Fill the remainder of the pot with soil.

Some potting mixes add water-absorbing crystals so you don't need to add more. Others contain slow-release fertilizer that eliminates the need to fertilize for part or all of the growing season. A sterile mix starts you off with a pest-free garden. None of us needs to buy any more problems than nature supplies free!

Once I have my pots, potting mix, and plants I like to set aside a few hours to assemble all my container gardens at once. Use a clean wheelbarrow to hold your potting mix. Empty the bags into the wheelbarrow, then simply scoop or shovel the needed soil into the pots. This is much easier and neater than pouring or scooping the mixture out of the bag. Use the wheelbarrow to move the soil to large planters. You may find it easier to fill and plant large containers where they are rather then moving them after they're planted and are much heavier.

A picnic table or makeshift bench can get the smaller pots to a better height for filling and viewing. Keeping materials, plants, soil and pots within easy reach makes it easier to spend an afternoon planting your container garden.

Cover the drainage holes with newspaper, coffee filter or a piece of weed barrier if you are concerned about losing soil. Don't add stones in the bottom of the container. It only adds weight and doesn't improve drainage. You can create a false bottom in larger pots to reduce amount of soil needed.

Fill the container with well-drained potting mix, about 4 to 6 inches from the upper edge. I like to mix a slow-release fertilizer into the soil if it doesn't already contain one. Incorporating a slow-release fertilizer now eliminates the need to fertilizer for most if not all of the season. Every time you water a little fertilizer is released. This eliminates messy mixing and the opportunity to procrastinate.

A pair of containers holding brightly colored marigolds are placed to be the perfect accent against the dark leaves of the Japanese maple.

An herb garden in varying terra cotta pots looks right at home in front of a wattle screen—notice the black stones used as mulch to give the pots an elegant finish.

This is also a good time to mix in water-retaining crystals. Some gardeners and professionals swear by these, while others find them less useful. Before adding them to the soil, make sure your potting mix does not already contain some. Adding more can create a slimy, smelly mess. Follow the label directions when adding moisture-retaining crystals. I once met a person who overdid the crystals when laying sod. As the crystals absorbed the moisture, the sod slid off the soil and down the hill. More is not always better.

Arrange the plants on the soil surface while they are still in their pots. This is the easiest way to fine-tune your design, though most gardeners have moved a few things around after planting. Most container gardens are packed full of plants. Since you control the water and fertilizer, it is easy to maintain more plants in a smaller space.

Get the best value out of each plant by selecting equally assertive plants and allowing enough space for them to grow.

The first time I grew sweet potato vine, I thought I needed three for my 24 inch container. Needless to say I had a pot full of sweet potato vines and a few surviving annuals buried under their foliage. Once you are happy with the arrangement of plants, carefully slide them out of their pots. Position them and add soil as needed so the plants are at the same depth as they were in their pots.

Rhythm and unity are achieved here by matching containers and plants with the same rounded shape as the surrounding rocks.

Once all the plants are in place, fill the container with soil. Gently tamp and water to remove air pockets and settle the soil. Add additional soil as needed. I like to cover the soil with fine mulch such as cocoa bean shells, evergreen needles, leaf mold or other organic material. Mulch softens the force of the water hitting the soil, helps conserve moisture, and dresses up the pot until the plants fill in.

Maintaining the Containers

Check containers daily for dryness, and water whenever the top few inches of soil are crumbly and moist. Water thoroughly so the excess runs out the bottom. Set the pots on a brick or use decorative pot "feet" to elevate the pots above the surface if they don't drain freely. That's one of the benefits of my old house—nothing is level, so all my pots drain easily when sitting on the uneven surfaces.

Adjust your watering schedule to your environment. The schedule will change with changes in the weather. High temperatures, bright sunlight and wind dry soil faster, and that means you'll need to water more often. Shady areas, cooler temps and high humidity

REDUCE WATERING

Even busy gardeners can enjoy container gardens. Reduce watering needs with these simple techniques:

- Incorporate water-absorbing crystals and gels that absorb water and hold it in the soil for plants to use.
- Line pots with sphagnum moss or water-absorbing mats made of materials like those used in disposable diapers.
- Invest in watering cones. These devices screw onto plastic one- and two-liter bottles. Fill the empty soda container with water, screw on the watering top, invert and place in the container. This no-waste system slowly delivers water to the plants' roots.

mean less work for you. The garden and its plants also influence watering schedule. Larger containers, pots made of materials that hold water, light colors that reflect heat, plants in shade, pots filled with drought-tolerant plants, and containers that are mulched need less water. Grouping plants also helps conserves moisture. As one plant transpires (equivalent to our sweating), the others benefit from the added humidity.

Self-watering pots may only need to be watered once or twice a week. Start by checking daily until you become familiar with how quickly the soil dries out and how often the reservoir needs refilling.

If you didn't plan ahead and have worn out a friendship or lack a plant-sitter, you may want to create your own self-watering system. Fill a 5-gallon pail with water. Run an absorbent wick of fabric or twine from the water-filled container into the soil of the plants you want to water. The soil will draw water from the pail through the wick. Use several wicks for larger containers. Secure the wick in the soil and in the water, and test out your system before leaving town. It may not be attractive but it certainly beats returning home to dead plants.

Or you can invest in a watering system. I have found small portable units that work on a timer and battery or electricity. You fill a large reser-

The containers are clearly the stars in this clever entry garden that reflects the style and architecture of the house.

voir with water and run thin tubes to each plant. The timer delivers water to the pots on a preprogrammed schedule. This system may be worth the money if you travel a lot or need a little help keeping your planters watered.

Look for other tools that make watering easy. Use a watering wand to extend your reach and deliver the water in a gentle spray. Consider purchasing one of the newer attachments with a crooked neck to make watering hanging baskets easier and drier. Balcony gardeners may want to invest in hoses that attach to indoor faucets, eliminating the need to haul water to the balcony.

Over time, watering washes the nutrients through the soil. Plus the soilless mixes do not hold onto nutrients the way mineral-based soils do. You won't need to fertilize for a while if your potting mix included a fertilizer or you added some at planting. Check the labels to find out when you should consider adding more. I find my container plants are robust and healthy when kept on a lean diet.

You can add slow-release fertilizer to the soil surface during the growing season if needed. Sprinkle the recommended amount according to label directions. Some benefit from light scratching into the surface, while others can rest on the soil surface.

Use water-soluble fertilizer if you need a quick fix of nutrients or enjoy fussing over your plants. These liquid or dry products are mixed with water and

Left: **A** beautiful container perfectly placed doesn't even need to hold any plants to play a starring role in this small garden.

Right: **N**ot only does this pink hibiscus match the pink accents on its container, but both highlight the pink garden furniture in the background.

This striking tower of potted sedges plays the role of statuary as a focal point in this garden.

Bulbs make a great addition to container gardens.

applied to the soil. Start with a dilute solution every other week or less if recommended by the manufacturer. Increase the frequency if your plants are not as robust as you like, or decrease if the plants are overgrown with healthy leaves and no blooms, or have browned leaves. Never use more than the recommended amount. Too much of anything can be harmful.

Special Additions

Bulbs make a great addition to container gardens. Their transient nature and need for chilling make them a bit more challenging. Gardeners in mild areas can plant them in their pots in fall as long as the soil temperature does not drop below freezing. Those in colder regions need to give the pots a bit of protection. Move the planted containers into an unheated garage, then place them on a board and surround with other materials for added insulation.

Or plant bulbs in smaller pots, water, and sink the pots in a vacant space in the garden or put them in a spare refrigerator. Look for ways to chill the bulbs if you are gardening in the south. Use varieties suited for warmer regions or store the bulbs in the refrigerator for 15 weeks to initiate bloom. Remove the bulbs from cold storage next spring and set in place.

Garden centers are making it easier for container gardeners. Purchase and plant precooled bulbs in spring. Mix them in with an existing planting or create a spring display using other cold-tolerant plants.

You can also purchase potted bulbs. Look for plants barely peeking through the soil so the plant has time to adapt to the brighter sun and colder temperatures outdoors. Set the bulbs pot and all into a window box or container garden to add a little color to your spring landscape.

Lift the bulbs or remove the pots when the bulbs have finished blooming, unless they are a permanent part of the container garden. Replace them with summer-flowering plants. You can do the same in fall, replacing faded summer annuals with flowering kale, mums or other fall beauties.

Edible Plants

Nothing beats fresh from the garden flavor, and you don't have to sacrifice it because of space limitations. Look at your favorite recipes and your available space to help you decide what to grow. Corn tastes great fresh from the

garden but doesn't give you the best return on investment in terms of the amount of produce for the space used. On the other hand, adding just one tomato plant to the landscape can supply many of your culinary needs. Create a vegetable garden in a pot or just mix a few veggies in with your flowers.

Scour the garden catalogues and the Internet to locate many of the new smaller varieties of vegetables. Their petite size and colorful fruits add beauty and edibility to any in-ground or potted garden. Tom Thumb and Patio are just two of the small tomatoes that need no support. Add a trellis and train taller tomatoes to be a vertical accent in your container garden. Try growing watermelon, pumpkins or squash in a pot and let the vines crawl around the edges of your patio or deck. Bush types are available for those who are even more space-challenged.

Don't forget about fruits and herbs. Use your favorite herbs to spice up your containers. Parsley, sage, thyme and others make nice fillers. Topiary rosemary trees are a beautiful statement in any garden and a tasty treat when you harvest the trimmings.

Columnar and dwarf apples, pears and citrus plants can be grown in containers. Northern gardeners will need to provide special winter protection to keep them alive through harsh winter. Kiwi and grapes can be grown in pots with trellises attached. Regular pruning will be needed to keep these

Raised planters make gardening easier for those who have trouble stooping and bending.

GROWING FRUIT TREES IN SMALL SPACES

Reserve a bit of space for your favorite fruit. A lemon tree in a pot, a living fence of carefully trained apples, or a pear tree espaliered against the wall can add beauty and some garden fresh produce for your family to enjoy.

Select a dwarf variety. Check on the mature size as dwarf only means smaller than the typical species. This can be much bigger than you think. Check height and width.

Look for self-fruitful varieties. These plants do not need a partner for cross-pollination and fruit formation. Otherwise you will need room for a pollinating variety in order to grow the fruit.

Identify over-wintering space for plants not container hardy in your area. This may be a sheltered spot outdoors, unheated garage, or a sunny window indoors.

vigorous growers in bound. Currants, elderberries and blueberries provide structure, fruit, fall color and interesting foliage. Plant a few strawberries in a pot and enjoy attractive foliage, pretty flowers and a few edible fruits.

Growing in pots allows you to push your hardiness limits. I know many a northern gardener growing figs and citrus in containers. They move the plants indoors for winter and outdoors for summer and usually harvest enough fruit to keep them happy.

Create your own jungle paradise by growing bananas, palms, jasmine and other tropical plants in pots. Try supplementing your outdoor plantings with a few houseplants from your indoor garden. Some gardeners plan ahead and propagate extra plants from their collection just for this purpose.

Some of you may be lucky enough to keep these plants outdoors year round, but check their hardiness or minimum temperature tolerances before leaving them out in the cold.

The rest of us will need to move these plants indoors for winter and grow them like houseplants. Some can be treated like cannas and elephant ears, allowed to go dormant and stored in a cool dark place.

This raised bed holds lettuces and strawberries for creating a colorful and edible groundcover.

Attracting the Wild Things

Add movement and color to your garden by attracting birds and butterflies. Include plants that provide nectar for butterflies and food for caterpillars. Phlox, nicotiana, zinnias, coneflower, trumpet vine and many other common

Nothing could be more inviting than these stepping stones through a pretty planting combining edibles with ornamentals.

COLD WEATHER CONTAINER CARE

Trees, shrubs and perennials are great additions to container gardeners. They add structure and form you just can't get with annuals. When planted in a pot, they do require extra protection to survive most of our winters. The roots are exposed to greater extremes and fluctuating soil temperatures due to the small, above-ground soil mass. Here are some options for successfully over-wintering container gardens.

Grow plants one or two zones hardier than your location. The roots of hardier plants are more likely to survive the winter in a pot.

Plant in large containers at least 2½ feet wide and deep. The larger the container, the more soil it holds for better root insulation.

Double pot so the inner container can be sunk in a vacant garden space for winter. Bury the container in the ground, water it, and mulch once the soil freezes. Lift the pot in spring and set it back in the decorative pot on the patio or balcony.

Move the container plantings to a sheltered location out of winter wind and winter sun, especially if the plants are evergreens. Place bales of straw around the container, cover the soil with woodchips, or otherwise insulate the roots for the winter ahead.

Store potted plants in an unheated garage. Place pots on boards set on cement for added insulation. Surround with insulating materials. Water whenever the soil is thawed and dry.

Grow the plants indoors in a sunny window at home or in your office. One friend had trouble moving his plants out in the spring—his office mates decided they liked all the added greenery.

Donate plants to a school or senior center with an atrium or greenhouse. They may have more space and have plenty of hands to care for and people to enjoy your growing gift.

Find a neighborhood greenhouse that rents space for over-wintering plants. These are few and far between, since most growers can't afford the risk of pests coming in with the plants.

landscape plants attract butterflies to your garden. And don't worry if you are 10 stories high—if you plant it they will come.

The same holds true for birds. Verbena, fuchsia, penstemon and other plants with tubular flowers provide nectar for small birds. With some seed-bearing plants such as coneflowers, sunflowers and grasses, you'll attract a wide arrange of winged wonders.

This elegant—and high maintenance—pathway sets off the surrounding planting of salad crops and flowers.

Add some shelter, water and a damp place for butterflies to congregate, and your small landscape will soon be filled with welcome guests. With a bird feeder and some ripe fruit for the butterflies, you can watch the numbers grow. Don't worry if you can't keep the feeders filled, the birds will survive. But keep your feeders full, and they will return on a regular basis.

This lovely kitchen garden proves it's possible to achieve both beauty and bounty in the same space.

Discovering Untapped Planting Space

Finding new places to plant is an ongoing process. I keep discovering patches of earth that need to be filled or planting techniques to help maximize my garden space. Some of my techniques came from years of growing vegetables on small sites and in short seasons. As I was looking for ways to maximize my garden's productivity, I found ideas that could be used in the ornamental garden as well.

Double up your plants. Mixing bulbs with perennials and annuals gives you extended bloom. Design your garden so both partners are in bloom at the same time for double the impact, or use plants that bloom at different times to extend the flowering time.

Try planting two perennials in the same hole. As the plants grow and mingle, you'll have double the bloom in the same location. Select plants with equal vigor, similar growing requirements and compatible size. If one plant

Don't overlook the space on the verge of the driveway for a small planting strip—this one is perfect for rock-garden plants.

overpowers the other, or one's blooms are overshadowed by the other's foliage, you have wasted a plant. If that happens, make a note in your journal—the best gardeners learn from their mistakes, and we all make plenty of them.

Select long-blooming plants with good-looking foliage. Include as many with year-round interest as possible. Extend the bloom time and year-round appeal with regular maintenance. I sometimes settle for fewer blooms when my schedule doesn't allow for the added maintenance. But when I can invest a bit of time in deadheading and grooming, I get longer-blooming, better looking plants. This is especially important when each individual plant counts as they do in a small garden.

Try some more intense pruning techniques such as espalier to fit large trees and shrubs into small spaces. Espalier them against a fence or wall, or use them to create a living fence or screen. Include some fruit trees for a tasty addition or flowering plants with good fall color and interesting bark for year-round appeal.

Managing the Garden's Mechanics

Small space gardens create challenges. Those with large landscapes can move utilitarian functions out of their hideaway and into another location. Those with only a balcony, patio or small lot have to find creative solutions for managing their resources.

When you garden, you create green debris. Most communities do not allow you to throw this in the garbage. Pest- and chemical-free green debris can be recycled right in the garden. Tuck damaged leaves, faded flowers

Left: **The space between the side of the house and the fence has been turned into a charming small brick-paved terrace garden.**

Right: **An even narrower side garden than in the previous photo has been put to beautiful use as a ribbon garden.**

ESPALIER

Make room for a tree or large shrub by pruning it to grow flat against a wall or training it along wires to create a narrow fence that changes throughout the year. Espalier takes some ongoing effort to do, but it is one way to get a big tree into a small space. Here are some basics to help you get started:

1. Locate the planting area and install wire supports on wall or posts if you are creating a fence. Make sure the support system is strong enough for the weight of the mature tree.

2. Prune the leader (main stem) back just above the second or third healthy bud above the first support during the first winter.

3. Next winter cut the leader back to just above the second or third bud above the second support.

4. Repeat until all tiers are formed

5. Train two side branches, one on each side, onto the support. Continue this each year until all tiers are covered or the desired pattern is achieved

6. Remove other side branches that appear.

7. Once the tree is established, remove any other laterals that form, shorten the side shoots off the established laterals to one leaf, and remove any stray branches.

Left: **A**n apple tree espaliered on a fence makes a lovely show in the spring.

Right: **I**n late summer, the ripening apples are easy to pick on an espaliered tree.

and similar clippings under your mature plants. They serve as mulch, conserving moisture, preventing weeds from sprouting and improving the soil as they break down.

Larger quantities of green debris require a bit more space for recycling. Small compost bins can be purchased or made. Tumbler-type composters are mounted on a structure. Place raw materials in the bin, turn occasionally and pour the compost into a garden cart. Standing bins made of preserved wood, plastic lumber, concrete reinforcing wire, or other durable materials can be tucked behind a garden, hidden by a section of fence or covered with a vine. Locate them so they are convenient to fill and empty.

Not enough room for these options? Contact your local municipality to find drop-off locations for leaves and other green debris. Or maybe your

If space permits, a composting area with straw bales for sides is inexpensive and environmentally friendly—the straw also gradually turns into compost.

gardening friends will trade a little yard waste management for some quiet time in your garden get-away.

Water is the other precious resource. It seems we either have too much, not enough or never at the right time. Spring floods and summer droughts are good reminders that nature controls the spigot. Containing and using rainwater in the landscape instead of allowing it to run into the street and storm sewers can save you money, improve your landscape, and recharge our groundwater supplies.

Gardeners around the world have been capturing and reusing rainwater for over 2000 years. As water prices rise, watering restrictions increase, and municipalities introduce storm water management policies, you may want to try rain barrels to capture the rain. You can capture over 600 gallons of water for every inch of rain that falls on 1,000 square feet of roof.

Don't let your small space garden prevent you from tapping into this wonderful resource. If you take a few minutes to peruse the Internet or page through some of the garden supply catalogs, you just might find a rain barrel for your garden. They come in a variety of colors and shapes and many are designed for small spaces.

Select a rain barrel with an automatic overflow device to prevent water from collecting near your foundation during a major rainstorm. Or use multiple interconnecting barrels to handle rainy periods and store larger quantities of rainwater. Make sure your barrel fits the available space, blends with your landscape design and can handle a reasonable amount of water.

Purchase or make a rain barrel with a cover to keep out insects and debris and with a spigot for easy emptying and use of collected water. These

Gardeners around the world have been capturing and reusing rainwater for over 2000 years.

CREATE YOUR OWN GARDENER'S GOLD

Even small space gardeners can recycle yard waste into compost. Simply place your green debris into a heap and let it rot. Yes, it really is as simple as that. The more effort you put into the process, the quicker you get results. Hide your compost pile behind a screen or tall plant. Or use a decorative bin that is an asset to your small landscape. Here are some tips to help speed the process.

- Create a pile at least 3 feet tall and 3 feet wide for quicker results.
- Add pest-free and pesticide-free plant debris, rinds, and kitchen scraps from fruits and vegetables.
- Sprinkle in a bit of fertilizer and moisten to the consistency of a damp sponge.
- Occasionally turn the pile to speed up decomposition.

You may worry about the smell, attracting animals, or the time needed to create compost. Here are some strategies to help you avoid or fix these problems.

- Avoid attracting animals to the compost pile— don't add meat, cheese or other animal products.
- Turn the pile or add dry materials if the composting materials become too wet and begin to smell.
- Speed up the process by shredding materials before placing them in the compost pile, by turning the compost pile, and by adding equal parts of fresh and dried materials.

Layering the contents of the compost bin aids the decay process.

are gravity fed and slow to empty. Run a soaker hose from the rain barrel to a nearby garden. Turn it on in the morning and let the water slowly drip into the soil while you are at work. Look for UV-resistant and cold-weather-tolerant materials. Northern gardeners will need to deal with ice issues by disconnecting or keeping the drain-ways ice-free much as you do gutters and downspouts.

Managing all your stuff can be as challenging as managing your garden's resources. Every gardener dreams of a beautiful shed complete with a potting station, shelves, room for all tools and equipment, and space to move around. Balcony gardeners just dream of a place to stow their furniture, potting mix, and a few small tools. As more gardeners move to apartments and condominiums, more and better storage options are becoming available.

Consider storage before purchasing outdoor furniture. Many benches of wood, resin and metal come with hidden storage areas beneath the seats.

Some are lined to hold ice so you don't have to find room for the cooler—just stand up and lift the lid when your guest needs a cold drink.

Evaluate how your furniture works in the space when not in use. Look for chairs and tables that can be folded and stored flat against the wall, or chairs that fold and can be stowed under a folding table. Hammocks are nice, but the frames often require more space than you can spare. Look for foldable frames, or built-in hooks or support structures that also can be used for other purposes.

Think about where you will put the furniture when the weather is too hot or cold to enjoy the outdoors. Select furniture suited to the sunlight, heat or cold in your area. Extend the life of your furnishings by storing them indoors or covering them during the off season.

Be sure to include a few of your favorite amenities. Small grills perfect for small spaces, outdoor reading lamps that make you feel as if you lifted the roof off your living room, sound systems and even televisions can blur the boundaries between your indoor and outdoor living space.

Now that the plants are in, plans are made for their care and feeding, and furniture and accessories are in place, you are ready to sit back relax and enjoy your garden retreat. And best of all—it is only a few steps from your back door.

With all the design, installation, and maintenance done, it's time to sit down and enjoy the garden.

Can't Miss
Small Space
Favorites

Selecting the plants to feature in a gardening book is about as difficult as selecting the plants to include in your landscape. I spent months agonizing over which plants to include, wanting to make sure I didn't offend any region or include troublesome plants. So I approached it like I was designing a garden. I thought about the important features of the plants I wanted to include

First they needed to fit into small spaces. That eliminated the larger shade trees that may be a part of the existing landscape but not the focus of this book. Then I looked for plants that provided several seasons of interest. I know as a small space gardener I am limited on the number of plants I can include, so the one selected better give me value throughout much of the year.

Then came the challenge of taking care of gardeners throughout a wide range of cold and heat zones. So I compromised. I selected plants that meet the needs of the widest range of gardeners. Those in the extreme cold and hot may need to look at the plants included here and find similar plants suited to their climate for their own small space. Also I grouped all the flowering plants together since some perennials are treated as annuals in colder parts of the country.

And now, a word on invasive plants. Some plants like butterfly bush are invasive in the Northeast and Northwest. Those in the Great Lakes region are grateful if their butterfly bushes live for a few years. I did my best to identify areas where certain plants are a problem so we don't contribute to the growing problem of invasive plants, while allowing gardeners to use these plants where they do not pose a threat. Always check with your local extension service and government websites such as the Plants Database at http://www.plants.usda.gov/, The Nation's Invasive Species Information System at http://www.invasivespeciesinfo.gov/, and the Information Management System for Invasive Plants at http://www.invasivespecies.org/ as the status of existing plants can change and new ones are introduced.

Fortunately the Horticulture profession is working with environmental groups to evaluate new plants before introducing them into the market place. It is better to avoid problems than create those that require lots of energy, money, and years to clean up.

As you look through the plant directory keep your landscape plan and notes on your growing conditions at hand. Look for plants that will thrive in your small space. A healthy plant will mean less work for you and will be a better-looking plant with greater impact for the space it occupies. Select plants hardy to your region. A USDA cold hardiness map is included in the back to help you determine your hardiness zone.

Keep in mind the information provided is general for each plant listed. Many have small varieties that are even better suited for small space gardens. In addition, hybridizers are developing new varieties with better flowers, more pest resistance, and other desirable features. The list keeps growing and the number of plants suited to your small space increases every season.

Make a list of the plants you think would work in your small space garden. Ask family and friends for their feedback. Now set the list aside for a few days. Revisit and evaluate the plant list before heading to the nursery or garden center. It is better to change your mind *before* purchasing and planting than after the plant has been hauled home and put in the ground.

Grab a cup of coffee or beverage of choice and get started selecting the right plant for your garden get away.

KEY TO ICONS

Along with each plant entry, you will notice small graphic icons. They convey additional useful information about the plant's characteristics or benefits. There are also icons indicating light requirements.

- attracts butterflies
- attracts hummingbirds
- produces edible plant parts
- has fragrance
- produces attractive fruit
- suitable for cut flowers
- long bloom period
- native plant
- supports bees
- provides food or shelter for wildlife
- good fall color
- drought resistant

- full sun
- part sun
- part shade
- full shade

Agapanthus
Agapanthus species
MATURE HEIGHT X SPREAD: 36 to 48 inches x 18 to 24 inches
HARDINESS: 7 to 10
USE: Spring flowering accent

Long lasting blue or white ball shaped flowers top green strappy foliage for a colorful spring display. The dark green leaves provide year round greenery making this plant a good addition to flower gardens and containers. The dwarf cultivar 'Peter Pan' is smaller in size with finer texture.

Agastache, Anise Hyssop
Agastache foeniculum
MATURE HEIGHT X SPREAD: 36 to 60 inches x 24 inches
HARDINESS: 5 to 9
USE: Summer to fall flowering accent

A heat resistant plant with fragrant foliage and spiky lavender flowers mid summer to fall. A well-known herb with anise scented leaves used in teas, salads and drinks. Grow in moist well-drained soils for best results. The 2003 All American selection winner 'Golden Jubilee' has golden foliage for added interest.

Ageratum
Ageratum houstonianum
MATURE HEIGHT X SPREAD: 6 to 20 inches x 6 to 12 inches
HARDINESS: Annual
USE: Summer-long colorful accent

Traditionally the blue of red white and blue gardens, ageratum blooms also come in white, violet and red hues. Use compact forms along a walk, in a small planter or as an edger for the flower bed. Try the taller 'Blue Horizon' to fill voids in the perennial garden and for cutting.

Allium, Ornamental Onion
Allium species
MATURE HEIGHT X SPREAD: 6 to 60 inches by 6 to 15 inches
HARDINESS: 2 to 10 (varies with species)
USE: Colorful accent

Purple, mauve, yellow or white round flowers add interest to the spring, summer or fall garden. Mix them with other perennials for a seasonal splash of color and bold statement in the garden. A brush of the foliage reveals its family ties to onion. Grow this bulb in well drained soils for best results.

Alyssum
Lobularia maritima
MATURE HEIGHT X SPREAD: 4 to 8 inches x 10 to 15 inches
HARDINESS: Annual
USE: Colorful ground layer

Use this traditional favorite for a season of color and fragrance. Plant them near steppers, in containers or mixed with other plants. The low growing plants are covered with white, pink, purple or apricot flowers that require little deadheading. Flowers best in cool temperatures and may reseed.

Amsonia
Amsonia species
MATURE HEIGHT X SPREAD: 24 to 48 inches x 18 to 48 inches
HARDINESS: 3 to 9
USE: Three season accent

A cluster of blue star shaped flowers top each stem in spring. The narrow green leaves turn a clear yellow for added color in the fall. Use this plant mixed with shrubs and other perennials. Avoid shade and fertile soils that lead to floppy growth.

Aster
Aster species
MATURE HEIGHT X SPREAD: 24 to 60 inches x 12 to 36 inches
HARDINESS: 3 to 10
USE: Fall and winter accent

Purple, white and pink flowers brighten the late summer and fall garden. Keep plants trimmed through June to promote compact growth and more flowers. Use them in containers or flowerbeds. Allow the plants to stand for winter to increase hardiness and for added interest in northern gardens.

Astilbe
Astilbe species
MATURE HEIGHT X SPREAD: 12 to 48 inches x 24 to 36 inches
HARDINESS: 3 to 9
USE: Colorful summer accent

The fluffy flower plumes of white, pink, lavender or red add color to the shadier spots of your garden getaway. The fern-like foliage provides season long greenery and the flowers are great in the garden or a vase. Leave late forming seed heads stand for winter interest.

Banana
Musa species
MATURE HEIGHT X SPREAD: 5 to 15 feet tall and 5 to 12 feet wide
HARDINESS: 8 to 10, grown as annual elsewhere
USE: Tropical accent, tree or screen

Bring a tropical feel to your garden by adding a banana plant or two. The large leaves provide shade and screen unwelcome views. Most gardeners must move the plants indoors for the winter. Grow them like a houseplant or store the rhizome in a cool dark location like a canna.

Bellflower

***Campanula* species**

MATURE HEIGHT X SPREAD: 6 to 36 inches x 6 to 36 inches
HARDINESS: 3 to 8
USE: Floral accent in late spring and early summer

Brighten up the late spring garden with a few bellflowers. Their blue, pink, lavender or white bell shaped flowers fill the flowering void between spring and summer bloomers. Select a variety that fits the available space and design of your garden.

Brugmansia, Angel's Trumpet

Brugmansia arborea* or *Datura arborea

MATURE HEIGHT X SPREAD: up to 8 to 14 feet x 10 feet
HARDINESS: 10 and 11, grown as annual elsewhere
USE: Focal point in the garden or container

Look but do not eat this poisonous beauty. One plant is all you need to add fragrance and interest to your small space garden. Most gardeners grow it as an annual or in a container to be wintered indoors. Plants flower summer and fall and older plants can be trained into a tree form.

Bugbane, Cohosh

Cimicifuga

MATURE HEIGHT X SPREAD: 3 to 7 feet by 2 feet
HARDINESS: 3 to 8
USE: Summer or fall flowering accent

Brighten the shade with the white candle-like flowers of bug bane. Use a combination of summer and fall blooming types for extended bloom. The green or purple fern-like foliage looks good all season and the seed pods add winter interest.

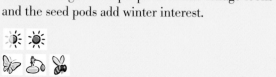

FLOWERS

Caladium
Caladium bicolor
MATURE HEIGHT X SPREAD: 1 to 24 inches x 12 to 24 inches
HARDINESS: 9 to 11, grown as annual elsewhere
USE: Season long color

Add a splash of color to the shade. Use caladiums with their colorful foliage in combinations of red, rose, pink, white, silver, bronze and green in gardens or containers challenged by shade. Grow as a house-plant indoors for winter or store the tubers in a cool dark place where not hardy.

Calendula, Pot Marigold
Calendula officinalis
MATURE HEIGHT X SPREAD: 3 feet x 18 inches
HARDINESS: Annual
USE: Summer through fall accent

Far south gardeners can use this as a winter annual while the rest of us enjoy the marigold-like yellow, orange and cream flowers summer through fall. They are pretty to look at and good to eat. Sprinkle a few flower petals on your summer salad. Grow them in the garden or a container.

California Poppy
Eschscholzia californica
MATURE HEIGHT X SPREAD: 6 to 12 inches tall and wide
HARDINESS: Annual
USE: Summer color accent

Brighten your small space with the orange, yellow, red and pink flowers of California poppy. The ferny foliage makes a nice backdrop for these summer bloomers. It is tolerant of adverse growing conditions and will reseed readily in mild regions.

Canna
Canna x *generalis*
MATURE HEIGHT X SPREAD: 12 to 84 inches x 18 to 24 inches
HARDINESS: 9 to 11, grown as annual elsewhere
USE: Tropical foliage and flowering accent

For some a traditional favorite, for others a new plant that provides the feel of the tropics. Canna's large green, bronze or variegated foliage provides a nice backdrop for the red, yellow, orange, pink or white flowers. Use tall ones for vertical accents in narrow spaces.

Coleus
Solenostemon scutellarioides
MATURE HEIGHT X SPREAD: 6 to 36 inches x 6 to 36 inches
HARDINESS: 10 and 11, grown as annual elsewhere
USE: Colorful foliage accent

Use coleus's colorful foliage in the garden or a container. Mix with other annuals or tuck a few in between perennials or under shrubs. The new sun tolerant cultivars extend the value of this plant beyond its shady past. Remove any flowers that appear and pinch back plants that may become leggy.

Coral Bells
Heuchera
MATURE HEIGHT X SPREAD: 4 to 30 inches x 5 to 24 inches
HARDINESS: 3 to 8
USE: Ground layer

Tuck this versatile perennial in with other plants or use it as a groundcover beneath a tree and shrub. Choose from green, purple, bronze or variegated foliage and coral, pink, white or green flowers early in the season. Provide bronze foliaged plants with a little afternoon shade.

Coreopsis
Coreopsis
MATURE HEIGHT X SPREAD: 8 to 30 inches x 8 to 24 inches
HARDINESS: 3 to 9
USE: Floral accent

Include a few of these sunny yellow flowers in your small space or container garden. These heat and mostly drought tolerant plants attract butterflies as they bloom throughout the summer. Try thread-leaved coreopsis for low maintenance long blooming flower.

Corydalis
Corydalis lutea
MATURE HEIGHT X SPREAD: 16 inches x 12 inches
HARDINESS: 4 to 9
USE: Long blooming Ground layer

A perennial you can love or hate. This low grower blooms non stop from spring through frost. The pale green foliage is topped with yellow tubular flowers that attract hummingbirds. The down side, it seeds around requiring a little weeding to keep it in bounds.

Cranesbill Geranium
Geranium sanguineum
MATURE HEIGHT X SPREAD: 8 to 15 inches x 24 inches
HARDINESS: 4 to 8
USE: Ground layer

Create a tapestry of color and texture at ground level using this and other low growing perennials. The foliage is covered with white, pink or lavender flowers in summer. Give it a haircut mid season to encourage fresh new growth then wait for the colorful fall foliage display.

Daffodil
Narcissus
MATURE HEIGHT X SPREAD: 6 to 24 inches x 6 to 12 inches
HARDINESS: 3 to 8
USE: Spring floral accent

Plant these once for years of spring flowers. Select from white, yellow, salmon, pink, green and combinations of these colors. Force a few in a pot for the patio or window box or tuck them in with your perennials. Mix them with daylilies to double the bloom and mask the daffodil leaves.

Daylily
Hemerocallis
MATURE HEIGHT X SPREAD: 1 to 4 feet x 2 to 3 feet
HARDINESS: 3 to 10
USE: ground layer or accent

Select a repeat bloomer for a season long bloom. Though the white, yellow, salmon, peach, orange, lavender, pink or purple edible flowers may only last a day, the profusion of flowers provides a long display. Use in a pot, as a groundcover or mixed with other flowers.

Delphinium
Delphinium elatum
MATURE HEIGHT X SPREAD: 3 to 6 feet x 2 feet
HARDINESS: 3 to 7
USE: Vertical accent

Add some charm with the stately blue, purple, white, red, pink and yellow summer flowers of larkspur. A strong vertical feature that reblooms in fall when fertilized and clipped back mid season. Reduce pest problems and increase hardiness by growing them in moist well-drained soil.

Elephant Ear
Colocasia and *Alocasia*
MATURE HEIGHT X SPREAD: 1 to 15 x 2 to 4
HARDINESS: 10, grown as annual elsewhere
USE: Foliage accent or screen

Select a small variety of elephant ears for containers and small plantings. Use larger varieties to create a living privacy screen. Most gardeners need to move the plants indoors for winter and grow as a houseplant or store the tuberous roots in a cool dark place.

Fan Flower
Scaevola aemula
MATURE HEIGHT X SPREAD: 20 inches x 20 inches
HARDINESS: 9 to 11, grown as annual elsewhere
USE: Ground layer

Allow this spreading annual to crawl across the ground as a groundcover or use it as an accent when planted in a container or hanging basket. The blue or white fan shaped flowers are present all season and the plant will survive a light frost.

Fern
Athyrium, Matteuccia, Osmundo, et al
MATURE HEIGHT X SPREAD: 4 to 48 inches x 8 to 36 inches
HARDINESS: 2 to 10
USE: Groundcover or foil

Lacy foliage provides a nice groundcover or a background for other shade loving flowers. Use ferns in pots or in the garden. The variety of leaf shapes, sizes and textures makes them useful in most garden designs. No shade, don't worry some are sun tolerant.

Flowering Tobacco
Nicotiana alata
MATURE HEIGHT X SPREAD: 10 to 60 inches x 6 to 24 inches
HARDINESS: 10 to 11 grown as annual elsewhere
USE: Floral accent

Use this free flowering plant to fill your small space with flowers, hummingbirds and butterflies by day and a sweet fragrance at night. Choose from white, pink, red, lavender, green and yellow flowers. Keep your eyes peeled for offspring as you prepare your garden next spring.

Fringed Bleeding Heart
Dicentra eximia
MATURE HEIGHT X SPREAD: 12 to 18 inches by 18 inches
HARDINESS: 3 to 9
USE: Ground layer

Consider using fringed bleeding heart as a groundcover or flowering accent. The fern-like foliage looks good all season when grown in full or part shade. The large burst of pink or white flowers appear in late spring or early summer and continue sporadically throughout the season.

Gaura
Gaura lindheimeri
MATURE HEIGHT X SPREAD: up to 5 feet x 3 feet
HARDINESS: 5 to 10
USE: Filler and floral accent

Try this long blooming perennial in hot dry locations where other plants have failed. Northern gardeners can grow these like annuals and enjoy a season of beautiful blooms. The airy texture and delicate white or pink flowers blend into most garden or container plantings.

Gayfeather
Liatris
MATURE HEIGHT X SPREAD: 1 to 6 feet x 1 to 2
HARDINESS: 3 to 9
USE: Colorful Vertical accent

Though native to the prairies this perennial is at home in formal and informal gardens. The purple or white spike flowers top stately stems summer through fall. Leave the plants with their fluffy seedheads stand for some winter interest and food for the birds.

Grape Hyacinth
Muscari
MATURE HEIGHT X SPREAD: 4 to 8 inches x 1 to 2 inches
HARDINESS: 2 to 8
USE: Spring blooming ground layer

Mix grape hyacinths in the lawn, perennial garden or force in a container. The foliage sprouts in fall and persists most of the year and tiny fragrant grape-like clusters of white or blue flowers appear in spring. Plant a spring "stream" of blue grape hyacinths for your small space.

Heliotrope
Heliotropium arborescens
MATURE HEIGHT X SPREAD: 12 to 18 inches by 12 to 15 inches
HARDINESS: 11, grown as annual
USE: Floral and fragrant accent

One plant can make a big impact in your small space. The wonderful fragrance and long lasting violet, purple or white flowers make a good addition to a container garden. Or plant some near a table or bench for all to enjoy the flowers and fragrance.

Hellebore, Lenten Rose
Helleborus x *hybridus*
MATURE HEIGHT X SPREAD: 18 to 24 inches x 24 inches
HARDINESS: 4 to 9
USE: Ground layer

Start your spring garden with the long lasting blossoms of hellebore. The flower color ranges from white to plum including reds, pinks and yellows. The spring blooms are followed by interesting seed pods and year round interest comes from its attractive evergreen foliage.

Hosta
Hosta
MATURE HEIGHT X SPREAD: 4 to 48 inches x 6 to 60 inches
HARDINESS: 3 to 9
USE: Ground layer

Tired of hostas? A second look is sure to reveal one to please you. The variety of new introductions in various sizes and variegated foliage makes them an eye-catching groundcover or shade plant. The spikes of white (sometimes fragrant) or lavender flowers can add to the show.

Hyacinth
Hyacinthus orientalis
MATURE HEIGHT X SPREAD: 6 to 12 inches x 6 inches
HARDINESS: 3 to 7, annual in zones 8 to 9
USE: Fragrant spring floral accent

Fill your small space with color and fragrance. Plant a few blue, violet, white, rose pink, yellow, salmon or apricot hyacinths in a pot or in the garden in fall for a spring display. Those in warmer locations will need to use precooled bulbs.

Impatiens
Impatiens walleriana
MATURE HEIGHT X SPREAD: 6 to 24 inches x 5 to 18 inches
HARDINESS: annual, perennial in zone 11
USE: Ground layer, floral accent

Create a colorful carpet or splash of color with shade tolerant impatiens. Select form white, orange, red, pink, violet, coral and yellow solid or bicolor flowers. Or plant a few in a pot for a colorful accent set on the patio, hung from the fence or hanging from a shepherds crook.

Iris
Iris
MATURE HEIGHT X SPREAD: 4 to 48 inches x 6 to 12 inches
HARDINESS: 3 to 10
USE: Floral accent spring and early summer

With a rainbow of colors and sizes to choose from, you are sure to find an iris suited to your small space garden. Use small ones near seating areas or forced in a pot and place on the table. Plant a few taller ones near a water feature or mixed in the garden for vertical interest.

Lady's Mantle
Alchemilla
MATURE HEIGHT X SPREAD: 3 to 20 inches x 15 to 24 inches
HARDINESS: 3 to 8
USE: Ground layer

Dress up the base of shrubs and trees or create a tapestry by mixing this with other groundcovers. The interesting foliage is topped by chartreuse flowers in late spring through early summer. Plant a few near a bench so you will be sure to see the morning dew collect on the leaf tips.

Lantana
Lantana
MATURE HEIGHT X SPREAD: 1 to 6 feet by 1 to 6 feet
HARDINESS: 9, grown as annual elsewhere
USE: Flowering accent

Attract a few butterflies and hummingbirds by planting a lantana in your small space. The colorful white, yellow, orange, red and pink flowers appear from summer through fall. Southern gardeners enjoy these flowers as shrubs while the rest of us include them as annuals.

Lily
Lilium species
MATURE HEIGHT X SPREAD: 2 to 6 feet tall x 1 to 3 feet
HARDINESS: 3 to 8
USE: Floral accent

Add a fragrant bouquet to the garden and cut a few for your favorite vase. The stately stems are topped with sometimes fragrant white, yellow, orange, red or pink flowers in summer. Buy precooled bulbs or force a few in an attractive container for the patio or deck.

Madagascar Periwinkle
Catharanthus roseus
MATURE HEIGHT X SPREAD: 6 to 24 inches by 12 to 24 inches
HARDINESS: 9 to 11, grown as annual elsewhere
USE: Ground layer

Fill a container or cover a space with the white, pink, rose, red or purple-red flowers of annual vinca. Heat, drought and pollution won't stop this plant from blooming all season long. The mounds of glossy green foliage and colorful flowers may remind you of impatiens.

FLOWERS

Mum
Chrysanthemum x *morifolium*
MATURE HEIGHT X SPREAD: 1 to 3 feet x 1 to 3 feet
HARDINESS: 3 to 9
USE: Fall floral accent

Freshen up the tired summer garden with white, yellow, orange, bronze, rust, red or lavender mums. Place a few potted mums at the entrance to welcome visitors or next to a bench or on the deck. Mix a few in with other perennials to extend your garden's bloom time.

Nasturtium
Tropaeolum majus
MATURE HEIGHT X SPREAD: 1 to 1 1/2 feet
    (8 feet for trailing varieties)
HARDINESS: Annual
USE: ground layer or vertical accent

Add a little spice to your favorite salad and color to the garden. Grow nasturtiums as an annual groundcover, on a trellis for screening or in a pot. The green or variegated foliage and the cream, yellow or orange or red flowers are attractive and edible.

Pansy
Viola x *wittrockiana*
MATURE HEIGHT X SPREAD: 4 to 8 inches x 12 inches
HARDINESS: Grown as summer or winter annual
USE: Fall through spring floral accent

Double your planting space and mask declining foliage by mixing pansies with spring flowering bulbs. Plant hardy cultivars such as 'Icicle' in fall for extended bloom. Southern gardeners will enjoy non stop bloom while northerners will need to wait for their return in spring.

Pentas
Pentas lanceolata
MATURE HEIGHT X SPREAD: 18 inches x 18 inches
    (larger where perennial)
HARDINESS: 8 to 11, grown as annual elsewhere
USE: Floral accent

Find space for a few of these long blooming flowers. The clusters of white, pink, rose or lilac flowers look great in a container or mixed with annuals and perennials in the garden. Plant them near a bench so you will be sure to spot the butterflies that stop by to sip their nectar.

Peony
Paeonia hybrids
MATURE HEIGHT X SPREAD: 3 to 5 feet x 3 to 5 feet
HARDINESS: 3 to 8
USE: Floral accent, seasonal shrub

Consider adding a traditional favorite, the peony, to your small space. One plant can give you three seasons of interest so place it where it can be enjoyed. Watch the spring foliage emerge with a tinge of red, followed by large, often fragrant, blossoms, lovely greenery turning reddish-purple in fall.

Petunia
Petunia x *hybrida*
MATURE HEIGHT X SPREAD: 6 to 18 inches x 6 to 36 inches
HARDINESS: Annual
USE: Summer or winter floral accent

Don't pass over petunias when looking for something new and different. You will be amazed by all the new varieties and tempted to try a few. Use the trailing types in hanging baskets or as groundcovers. Mix them with sweet potato vine or other plants for an updated look.

Phlox
Phlox species
MATURE HEIGHT X SPREAD: 3 to 48 inches x 24 inches
HARDINESS: 3 to 9
USE: Ground layer or floral accent

Use creeping phlox as a groundcover, woodland phlox to transition from spring to summer garden and the taller garden phlox for vertical accent in sunny locations. Select a mildew resistant phlox with the bloom time and growth habit suited to your small space garden.

Russian Sage
Perovskia atriplicifolia
MATURE HEIGHT X SPREAD: 3 to 6 feet x 2 to 3 feet
HARDINESS: 4 to 9
USE: Vertical accent

Plant some year round interest in your small garden. Russian sage's gray-green fragrant foliage combines well with other sun lovers. The blue flowers appear midsummer and are effective through fall. Leave the plant stand for winter cutting them down to 4 to 6 inches in late winter.

Salvia
Salvia x *superba*
MATURE HEIGHT X SPREAD: 24 to 36 inches x 24 inches
HARDINESS: 3 to 8
USE: Summer Floral Accent

Grow a few perennial salvias for you, the hummingbirds and butterflies to enjoy. Pinch or snip off faded blooms to keep the plants blooming throughout the summer. A midseason prune will keep plants tidy and encourage flowers and the winged wildlife to return.

Scarlet Sage
Salvia splendens
MATURE HEIGHT X SPREAD: 8 to 30 inches x 8 to 15 inches
HARDINESS: 10,11 Grown as annual elsewhere
USE: Floral accent

Liven up your small space with colorful annual salvia. The bright red flowers steal the show and need some equally powerful colors for balance. Or tone it down with more subtle blues, violets, salmon, white pink and lavender. Works well in the garden or a pot.

Sedum
Sedum
MATURE HEIGHT X SPREAD: 2 to 24 inches x 6 to 24 inches
HARDINESS: 3 to 8
USE: Ground layer

Plant them in the ground, between boulders in a retaining wall, a pot or anywhere you have a bit of soil in the sun. This large group of perennials offers a bit of everything for the garden. Interesting foliage, flowers, fall color on some and winter interest provided by others.

Solomon's Seal
Polygonatum
MATURE HEIGHT X SPREAD: 1 to 6 feet x 1 to 2 feet
HARDINESS: 3 to 9
USE: Groundcover or architectural accent

Add Solomon's seal to a container or shady corner of the garden. Use the variegated variety to brighten the shade. Highlight the large arching stems for added interest. Watch for the greenish-white bell shaped flowers in late spring followed by the blueberries.

FLOWERS

Sweet Potato Vine
Ipomoea batatas cultivars
MATURE HEIGHT X SPREAD: 3 to 15 feet long
HARDINESS: 9 to 11, grown as annual elsewhere
USE: Ground layer or trailing plant

Cover the ground, fill a container or screen a view with the trailing foliage of sweet potato vine. 'Marguerite' is the most popular and robust of the cultivars. Try vigorous 'Blackie' for dark purple foliage or the timid 'Tricolor' with cream, green and pink leaves.

Tulip
Tulipa species
MATURE HEIGHT X SPREAD: 6 to 36 inches x 6 inches
HARDINESS: 4 to 7, annual in warmer areas
USE: Spring floral accent

Welcome spring to your garden retreat with a few strategically placed tulips. Place a pot of forced tulips on the deck, table or patio for an added touch of color. Or mix them in with perennials to double your planting space extend the bloom time in the garden.

Verbena
Verbena x *hybrida*
MATURE HEIGHT X SPREAD: 8 to 12 inches x 20 inches
HARDINESS: Annual
USE: ground layer floral accent

Add some color to the ground layer of your small space by adding some of the white, lavender, purple, blue, pink, red or apricot verbena. Or grow them in a pot mixed with other plants. No matter where you put them they will brighten your small space from summer through fall.

Yarrow
Achillea species
MATURE HEIGHT X SPREAD: 6 to 52 inches x 12 to 24 inches
HARDINESS: 3 to 9
USE: Floral accent

Grow your own cut flowers in your small space. Add a heat tolerant yarrow plant to a sunny spot in the garden. Enjoy the yellow, white, pink or red flowers in the garden or indoors in a vase. Select smaller less invasive cultivars for the garden.

Yucca
Yucca filamentosa
MATURE HEIGHT X SPREAD: 2 to 3 feet (foliage) x 5 feet
HARDINESS: 4 to 10
USE: Foliage accent

Add a bit of southwest flare to any garden by including a yucca. The green or striped sword like foliage provides year round color. The flowers appear in summer rising 4 feet or more above the plant. Watch for hummingbirds nectaring on the white bell shaped flowers.

Zinnia
Zinnia elegans
MATURE HEIGHT X SPREAD: 6 to 36 inches x 8 to 12 inches
HARDINESS: Annual
USE: Floral accent

Bring in the butterflies and fill your vases with this heat loving annual. They come in a wide range of colors from green to red, pink, salmon, yellow, orange, white, and violet and grow well in the garden or container. Use mildew resistant cultivars.

GROUNDCOVERS

Barrenwort
Epimedium x *rubrum*
MATURE HEIGHT X SPREAD: 8 to 12 inches x 8 to 12 inches
HARDINESS: 4 to 8
USE: Groundcover with Year Round interest

Dress up the ground layer year round with barrenwort. The red, yellow or white flowers appear in early spring as the new growth emerges. The heart shaped leaves are tinged red as they emerge in spring, turn green and then red for fall and winter.

Bugleweed
Ajuga reptans
MATURE HEIGHT X SPREAD: 6 to 9 inches x 24 to 36 inches
HARDINESS: 3 to 9
USE: Groundcover

Cover bare areas and crowd out unwanted weeds with this plant. The solid green, bronze, or variegated foliage create a dense mat. Blue flower spikes appear in spring for added interest. Interplant with hosta for double the flowering and foliage interest.

Deadnettle
Lamium maculatum
MATURE HEIGHT X SPREAD: 8 to 12 inches x 36 inches
HARDINESS: 4 to 8
USE: Groundcover for dry shade

Brighten up shady areas with deadnettle. The variegated foliage lightens even those dark areas under Norway maples and oak trees. The rose-purple or white flowers provide added color from late spring into early summer.

146

CAN'T MISS SMALL SPACE GARDENING

Ginger
Asarum species
MATURE HEIGHT X SPREAD: 6 to 12 inches x 12 inches
HARDINESS: 4 to 9
USE: Evergreen or Deciduous Groundcover for Shade

Crush a leaf and take a whiff to discover the source of this plant's common name. Canadian ginger is native to the United States and tolerates dense shade even that found under evergreens. The glossy evergreen foliage of European ginger can be a bit more difficult for northern gardeners to establish.

Kinnikinnick, Bearberry
Arctostaphylos uva-ursi
MATURE HEIGHT X SPREAD: 4 inches x 24 inches
HARDINESS: 2 to 6
USE: Groundcover with seasonal interest

Create seasonal change at ground level with bearberry. Its green leaves make a great backdrop for the white and pink spring flowers. Red berries appear in fall and persist into winter. Watch the leaves change to gold tipped in red. Southern gardeners should consider A. x media hardy in zones 7 to 9.

Lilyturf
Liriope species
MATURE HEIGHT X SPREAD: 8 to 12 inches x 12 to 18 inches
HARDINESS: 4 to 11
USE: Flowering groundcover

Fill vacant areas with grass-like clumps of lily turf. Enjoy the spikes of white or purple flowers in summer that top the evergreen or semi-evergreen foliage. Southern gardeners may be tired of this groundcovers while those in the north struggle to add this beauty to their small spaces.

GROUNDCOVERS

Mother of Thyme
Thymus serpyllum
MATURE HEIGHT X SPREAD: 3 to 6 inches x 18 inches
HARDINESS: 4 to 9
USE: Fragrant groundcover

Surround steppers with a bit of this fragrant greenery. As your feet brush over the thyme they release a bit of fragrance into your small space. Great for hot dry areas this is a great substitute for grass. Plus the purple blooms in summer add to its over all appeal.

Sweet Woodruff
Galium odoratum
MATURE HEIGHT X SPREAD: 6 to 8 inches x 24 inches
HARDINESS: 4 to 8
USE: Fragrant flowering groundcover

Take a deep breath on a warm summer evening and you will enjoy the fragrance of this groundcover. The fragrant leaves cover the ground spring through fall. The dainty white flowers appear in late spring. Add a sprig or two of leaves and flowers to flavor your own May wine.

Vinca, Periwinkle
Vinca minor
MATURE HEIGHT X SPREAD: 6 inches x 24 inches and more
HARDINESS: 4 to 9
USE: Evergreen groundcover

Dress up those bare areas with vinca. The green or variegated foliage persists all year. Watch for the blue, dark blue or white flowers in spring. Mix in a few autumn crocus (*Colchicum*) for a surprise fall bloom. Check before planting as this plant is invasive in some areas.

Blue Fescue
Festuca cinerea
MATURE HEIGHT X SPREAD: 6 to 10 inches x 10 inches
HARDINESS: 4 to 8
USE: Groundcover, accent

Surround your favorite garden statue, cover a bare patch of earth or mix it with annuals in a pot or perennials in the garden. The tuft of narrow blue foliage is topped with blue-green flowers followed by beige seed heads in summer. Leave this grass stand for added winter interest.

Feather Reed Grass
Calamagrostis acutiflora 'Stricta'
MATURE HEIGHT X SPREAD: 4 to 5 feet x 2 feet
HARDINESS: 4 to 8
USE: Short screen or vertical accent

Screen the compost bin, provide a vertical accent next to water or mix this ornamental grass with other perennials. The narrow growth habit provides height while taking up minimal space. The pink flowers appear in summer followed by beige seed heads and foliage that persist all winter.

Hakonechloe
Hakonechloa macra cultivars
MATURE HEIGHT X SPREAD: 20 to 24 inches x 20 to 24 inches
HARDINESS: 4b to 9
USE: Grass accent for shade

Combine hakone grass with the bold foliage of a blue leafed hosta for a can't miss shade combination. The green and cream striped foliage is tinged pink in the fall. The flowers are light and airy tinged pink appearing in late summer. Enjoy the added interest or remove the flowers to keep the foliage the star.

ORNAMENTAL GRASSES

Miscanthus, Silver Grass
Miscanthus sinensis
MATURE HEIGHT X SPREAD: 3 to 7 feet x 4 feet
HARDINESS: 4 to 9
USE: Screening and vertical accent

Use taller varieties of silver grass for the walls of your small get-away or to screen a bad view. Combine shorter varieties with perennials or annuals for year round interest. The fluffy seed heads appear late summer or fall and persist through the winter. Avoid varieties invasive in your region.

Moor Grass, Purple Moor Grass
Molinia caerulea
MATURE HEIGHT X SPREAD: Foliage is 1 to 3 feet x 1 to 2 feet
HARDINESS: 4 to 9
USE: Airy screen or vertical accent

Create an airy screen, soften a nearby structure or create some winter interest. The shorter tufts of leaves are topped by 4 to 7 feet flower stems in mid summer. The panicles of purple flowers and foliage turn yellow for the fall. Some winter interest but other features make it worthy of some space in your garden.

Muhly Grass
Muhlenbergia capillaris
MATURE HEIGHT X SPREAD: 3 to 5 feet x 2 to 3 feet
HARDINESS: 7 to 11
USE: Year round foliar accent

Increase the fall beauty of your small garden with muhly grass. The narrow bright green leaves are topped with airy pink to purple flowers in the fall. Its fine texture blends well with other plants in both formal and informal settings. Northern gardeners may want to substitute hardy fountain grass.

Prairie Dropseed
Sporobolus heterolepsis
MATURE HEIGHT X SPREAD: 3 to 3$^1/_2$ feet x 2 to 3 feet
HARDINESS: 3 to 9
USE: Foliar accent

Use this native prairie in formal or informal settings. The narrow green leaves are topped with delicate pale pink flowers followed by beige seed heads. Watch the light glisten on ice crystals that form on the seed heads. Enjoy the yellow-orange fall color and let the plants stand all winter.

Purple Love Grass
Eragrostis spectabilis
MATURE HEIGHT X SPREAD: 2 feet x 2 feet
HARDINESS: 5 to 9
USE: Foliar accent

Welcome fall into your small space with a burst of color from purple love grass. A cloud of reddish purple flowers appear in fall. Soon the narrow green leaves acquire a reddish tinge adding to the fall interest. Use this plant to create a focal point for the fall garden.

Sedge
Carex species
MATURE HEIGHT X SPREAD: 6 to 60 x 10 to 36 feet
HARDINESS: 3 to 9
USE: Ground layer, foliage

Here's the perfect grass-like plant for those wet areas. Most sedges are native to wet areas in full sun or shade. Use them as a groundcover, accent in a container or contrasting foliage to the hostas, ginger and other commonly used shade plants.

SHRUBS

Arborvitae
Thuja occidentalis cultivars
MATURE HEIGHT X SPREAD : Varies greatly with cultivar
HARDINESS : 2 to 8
USE : Screening, divider, accent

Incorporate one of the new colorful cultivars as an accent among other shrubs or perennials. Or use one of the shorter upright varieties as a screen to create your garden get away. The many new varieties give this traditional plant a new look increasing its landscape appeal.

Beautyberry
Callicarpa species
MATURE HEIGHT X SPREAD : 4 to 6 feet x 4 to 6 feet
HARDINESS : 5 to 10
USE : Divider, accent

Brighten the fall garden with the eye-catching fruit of beautyberry. The purple fruit cover the stems in fall and persist several weeks after the leaves turn a pinkish purple to almost a lavender and drop. The less showy pink or white flowers appear in summer.

Blueberry
Vaccinium species
MATURE HEIGHT X SPREAD : 2 to 12 x 3 to 8 feet
HARDINESS : 3 to 9
USE : Divider, accent

Grow your own blueberries while adding seasonal interest to your small space. The lovely white, often tinged pink, flowers appear in spring before the leaves. The edible fruit ripens in summer and the orange to red fall color tops off the seasonal display. Plants need moist well-drained acid soil.

Blue Spirea, Bluebeard
Caryopteris x *clandonensis*
MATURE HEIGHT X SPREAD : 3 feet x 3 feet
HARDINESS : 5 to 9
USE : accent, low divider

Paint your late summer garden blue with the flowers of these plants. The mounded growth habit makes it easy to blend with other perennials and shrubs. Leave the seed heads on the plants for winter interest then cut the plant back to 4 to 6 inches in late winter.

Boxwood
Buxus microphylla
MATURE HEIGHT X SPREAD : 3 to 4 feet x 3 to 4 feet
HARDINESS : 4 to 9
USE : Screen, divider

Divide your hideaway into smaller spaces, create a backdrop for your flowers or add year-round greenery by adding boxwood to your garden. A shade-tolerant evergreen at home in a formal or informal setting. Protect these plants in the north from drying winter winds and sun.

Camellia
Camellia sasanqua
MATURE HEIGHT X SPREAD : 6 to 10 feet x 4 to 10 feet
HARDINESS : 7 to 9
USE : Screen

Add some winter color to your southern small space garden. The white, pink, rose, or red flowers cover the evergreen foliage. Grow in a protected site and expect some flower damage in zone 7. Those gardening further north will need to visit these plants at your local conservatory.

SHRUBS

Clethra, Summersweet
Clethra alnifolia
MATURE HEIGHT X SPREAD : 3 to 8 feet x 4 to 6 feet
HARDINESS : 3 to 9
USE : Summer flowering accent, divider, screen

Freshen the summer landscape with the sweet fragrance of summer-sweet. Its fragrant white flowers appear in summer and last for 4 to 6 weeks. The yellow to rich golden brown fall foliage provides a colorful finale for the season. This adaptable plant prefers acidic organic soils and tolerates wet conditions and shade.

Cotoneaster
Cotoneaster species
MATURE HEIGHT X SPREAD : 1 to 12 feet x 3 to 8 feet
HARDINESS : 3 to 8
USE : groundcover, screen, specimen

Increase year round interest in your small garden. Include a cotoneaster for the white, pink or rose flowers in spring. The red or black fruit follow providing some color and food for the birds. Some are evergreen while others give a colorful foliage show of purplish-red in fall before they drop.

Daphne
Daphne
MATURE HEIGHT X SPREAD : 1 to 4 x 1 to 4 feet
HARDINESS : 4 to 9
USE : focal point, screen, groundcover

Add a bit of fragrance to your spring landscape with one of the daphnes. Their fragrant white, rosy-purple or pink flowers cover the plant in late winter or spring. Several have variegated foliage for add interest. Select one that fits the space, landscape design and is hardy to the area.

Fothergilla
Fothergilla gardenii
MATURE HEIGHT X SPREAD : 2 to 4 feet x 2 to 4 feet
HARDINESS : 4 to 9
USE : Screen, focal point

Start the season with a bit of fragrance and end it with a colorful foliar display. Fothergilla's white flower look like bottle brushes and last for about 2 weeks in spring. The fall color develops late but the combination of yellow, orange and red is worth the wait

Hibiscus
Hibiscus rosa-sinensis
MATURE HEIGHT X SPREAD : 4 to 10 feet x 4 to 6 feet
HARDINESS : 9 to 11
USE : Screen, divider, accent

Bring the tropics to your small space with the colorful hibiscus. Single or double flowers of white, yellow, peach, orange or red appear throughout the summer. Use several to create a screen or one plant as a focal point. Northern gardeners will need to winter them indoors as a houseplant.

Holly
Ilex species
MATURE HEIGHT X SPREAD : varies with variety
HARDINESS : 3 to 10
USE : Screen, divider

Provide some food and shelter for the birds and a bit of color for the winter garden. Select form the wide range of evergreen and deciduous hollies. The glossy green leaves of some and red berries on all the female plants will provide welcome color in the winter garden.

SHRUBS

Hydrangea
Hydrangea species
MATURE HEIGHT X SPREAD : 3 to 15 feet x 3 to 15 feet
HARDINESS : 3 to 9
USE : Screen, Focal point

Brighten a shady location with the white summer flowers of smooth hydrangea. Or add some blue and pink color to the summer garden with the bigleaf hydrangea, great fall color from the oakleaf hydrangea or late season bloom on the bigger panicled hydrangea. Select the one best for your landscape design.

Juniper
Juniperus species
MATURE HEIGHT X SPREAD : Size and shape varies
HARDINESS : 2 to 9
USE : Evergreen groundcover, screen, focal point

Fill a hot dry spot in your small space with one of the interesting juniper cultivars. Select from narrow upright, spreading, and ground hugging forms. The evergreen foliage varies from medium green, bright green, blue-green and cream, yellow or apricot tipped. Their heat and drought tolerance makes them easy care plants.

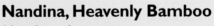

Nandina, Heavenly Bamboo
Nandina domestica
MATURE HEIGHT X SPREAD : 6 to 8 feet x 6 to 8 feet
HARDINESS : 6 to 9
USE : Divider, accent

Add texture and color with this ornamental shrub. Nandina produce creamy white flowers in late spring even when grown in the shade. The showy red fruit appear in fall and persist all winter. Prune to prevent leggy growth and avoid using this in areas where it is invasive.

Pyracantha, Firethorn
Pyracantha coccinea
MATURE HEIGHT X SPREAD : 6 to 18 feet x 6 to 18 feet
HARDINESS : 5 to 9
USE : Screen, divider, groundcover

Brighten the winter landscape with the orange-red berries of firethorn. The glossy green leaves are evergreen in most areas and white flowers are quite showy in spring. Train it up a wall, espalier on a support or just prune regularly to keep it in bound. But watch out for the thorns.

Rhododendron, Azalea
Rhododendron species
MATURE HEIGHT X SPREAD : 5 feet x 3 to 5 feet
HARDINESS : 4 to 8
USE : Flowering screen or divider, focal point

Start off the season with the red, purple, pink, white, yellow or orange blossoms of azaleas and rhododendron. Select a deciduous or evergreen variety suited to your climate. Plant in moist well-drained soil in a protected spot out of the winter wind and sun for best wintering success and spring flowering.

Rose
Rosa species
MATURE HEIGHT X SPREAD : 1 to 15 feet x 3 to 15 feet
HARDINESS : 2 to 8
USE : Flowering groundcover, screen, dividers

Add four seasons of interest to your garden get-away. Plant one of the hybrid tea, shrub or miniature roses hardy to your area. The summer long blooms of white, pink, red, yellow, orange, lavender or similar hues are followed by red or orange rose hips that persist through winter.

SHRUBS

Rose-of-Sharon
Hibiscus syriacus
MATURE HEIGHT X SPREAD : 8 feet x 5 feet
HARDINESS : 5 to 8
USE : Screen, vertical accent

End the summer with the white, red, purple or violet flowers of this plant. The hibiscus flowers appeal to many gardeners. Use this upright shrub as a screen or vertical accent in the small garden. Prune heavily in late winter or early summer every couple years to encourage large blooms.

Viburnum
Viburnum species
MATURE HEIGHT X SPREAD : 2 to 15 feet x 2 to 10 feet
HARDINESS : 2 to 9
USE : Screen, divider, focal point

Add some year round interest to your small landscape with a viburnum. Their white spring flowers may be fragrant, smelly or just pretty to view. The foliage may be evergreen or deciduous and many viburnums have fruit the birds love to eat or we can enjoy throughout the winter. Don't miss the outstanding fall color.

Weigela
Weigela florida
MATURE HEIGHT X SPREAD : 2 to 6 feet x 2 to 12 feet
HARDINESS : 4 to 9
USE : Screen, divider, accent

Check out all the new and interesting varieties of this traditional garden favorite. Small cultivars make them perfect for most small spaces. The foliage may be green, bronze or variegated and the pink, red, white or rose flowers appear from late spring and sporadically through the summer.

Citrus
Citrus
MATURE HEIGHT X SPREAD: 8 to 25 feet x 3 to 10 feet
HARDINESS: 9 to 11
USE: specimen plant, framework of garden

Grow in a pot on the patio or incorporate into your permanent plantings in mild climates. Most gardeners will need to overwinter these tender plants indoors like a houseplant The hassles of moving the plants will be rewarded with fragrant white flowers in the spring.

Crabapple
Malus hybrids
MATURE HEIGHT X SPREAD: 8 to 20 feet x 10 to 15 feet
HARDINESS: 4 to 9
USE: Canopy, framework

Take time to pick the perfect crabapple for your garden. There are hundreds of various sizes, shapes with white, pink or rose flowers and yellow to orange or red fruit. Select the form that fits your space and design. Reduce your work load by selecting a disease resistant cultivar.

Crape Myrtle
Lagerstroemia indica
MATURE HEIGHT X SPREAD: 15 to 20 feet x 10 feet
HARDINESS: 7 to 9
USE: Canopy, framework

Add a crape myrtle for year round interest. The crinkly flowers of white, lavender, pink, coral or red dress up the tree from late summer through fall. The green leaves turn an attractive golden yellow each fall before dropping to show off the peeling bark that exposes streaks of brown and maroon.

Dogwood
Cornus
MATURE HEIGHT X SPREAD: up to 20 feet x 10 feet or more wide
HARDINESS: 3 to 9
USE: Specimen, framework

Look for a tree form of dogwood that is hardy to your area and fits the space and landscape design. The flowering dogwood with its white or pink bracts is the showiest but the Pagoda, Kousa and Cornelian cherry dogwoods also provide seasonal interest with flowers, fruit and fall color.

Japanese Maple
Acer palmatum
MATURE HEIGHT X SPREAD: 3 to 20 feet tall and wide
HARDINESS: 5 to 8
USE: Specimen, canopy, framework

Create your own Japanese garden or just incorporate the beauty of the Japanese maple into your garden get-away. The deeply lobed leaves come in green, red-purple or variegated forms that turn yellow or orange in fall. Varieties with dissected foliage add a lacy delicate feature to the garden.

Magnolia
Magnolia
MATURE HEIGHT X SPREAD: up to 15 feet tall and wide
HARDINESS: 3 to 9
USE: Specimen, canopy, framework

Wake up your spring garden with the fragrant blooms of a small scale magnolia. The white, pink or yellow blooms signify the start of the growing season for many gardeners. The thick leathery green leaves are great for screening and the smooth gray bark brightens the winter landscape.

Musclewood

Carpinus caroliniana

MATURE HEIGHT X SPREAD: up to 30 feet x 30 feet
HARDINESS: 3 to 9
USE: Canopy, framework

Include this native in your formal or informal garden. This slow growing shade tolerant tree is perfect for a small space. The yellow, orange or red fall color adds a splash of color to your garden get a way. Its smooth gray bark and persistent seed capsules add to the winter appeal.

Redbud

Cercis canadensis

MATURE HEIGHT X SPREAD: up to 20 feet x 20 feet
HARDINESS: 4 to 9
USE: Specimen, Canopy, Framework

Get great impact in your small hide away from one small tree. The redbud starts its growing season covered with rosy pink flowers in early spring and ends the season with clear yellow fall color. Winter reveals a unique shape and the subtly attractive orange and brown bark.

Serviceberry

Amelanchier

MATURE HEIGHT X SPREAD: 5 to 20 feet or more tall and wide
HARDINESS: 2 to 9
USE: Specimen, Framework, Canopy

Include a tree or shrub form of this great four season plant. The season begins with white flowers, followed by small pink turning to blue fruit in June, then yellow, orange or red fall color and smooth gray bark that stands out in the winter landscape. The fruit is edible but the birds usually beat you to the harvest.

VINES

Clematis
Clematis
MATURE HEIGHT X SPREAD: 5 to 18 feet x 3 feet
HARDINESS: 4 to 9
USE: Screen, walls, vertical interest

Screen a bad view or use a clematis clad fence to create your garden hideaway. This fast growing twining vine provide a flowering wall of foliage with morning sun, cool soils and minimal care from you. The white, pink, red, purple, blue or yellow flowers appear in spring, summer or fall.

Climbing Hydrangea
Hydrangea anomala petiolaris
MATURE HEIGHT X SPREAD: 60 to 80 feet x size of support
HARDINESS: 4 to 9
USE: Screen, walls for shade

Soften a brick wall or other masonry structure with this four season vine. Watch for the slightly frangrant white flowers in early summer, yellow fall color and orange peeling bark that is revealed once the leaves drop for winter. These stems attach by aerial rootlets and should not be grown on wood or vinyl siding.

Climbing Rose
Rosa
MATURE HEIGHT X SPREAD: 6 to 30 feet x 3 to 6 feet
HARDINESS: 2 to 8
USE: Screen, Canopy

Add a little fragrance and color as you create the walls and canopy of your garden get-away. Train a climbing rose on a fence, trellis or arbor for shade. Select a pest resistant variety hardy to your area and one with the flower color (red, white, pink, yellow or orange) and fragrance you desire.

Honeysuckle Vine
Lonicera
MATURE HEIGHT X SPREAD: 12 feet or more x size of support
HARDINESS: 4 to 8
USE: Screen, canopy

Attract a few hummingbirds to your garden with the help of this twining vine. Orange-red or red trumpet shaped blossoms appear throughout the summer and into fall. Many are lightly scented so plant where you can sit and enjoy the fragrance and visiting hummers. Avoid varieties that are invasive in your area.

Hyacinth Bean
Lablab purpureus
MATURE HEIGHT X SPREAD: 10 to 12 feet x 1 to 2 feet
HARDINESS: 10,11 grown as annual elsewhere
USE: Annual screen, vertical accent

Quickly cover a trellis or fence or create a screen for the season. The twining stems of hyacinth bean vine produce white or purple flowers and attractive red-purple seedpods from summer through fall. This is typically grown as an annual but can occasionally reseed.

Jasmine, Confederate or Star Jasmine
Trachelospermum jasminoides
MATURE HEIGHT X SPREAD: 3 to 15 feet x 3 feet or more
HARDINESS: 6 to 10
USE: Fragrant screen

Use these twining and rambling vines on trellises or arbors where their fragrant white flowers can be enjoyed. Prune every few years to keep it contained in milder regions. Northern gardeners can grow them in a pot outside for the summer and bring it indoors for the winter.

Mandevilla
Mandevilla
MATURE HEIGHT X SPREAD: 10 to 20 feet x 1 to 3 feet
HARDINESS: 10 to 11, grown as annual elsewhere
USE: vertical accent

Include this flowering vine in your small space. The pink to red or white flowers last several days but the floral display lasts all season. Watch for flowers year round if you live in a mild climate. Ambitious gardeners can move mandevilla indoors for the winter.

Morning Glory
Ipomoea pupurea or I. tricolor
MATURE HEIGHT X SPREAD: 6 to 12 feet x 1 to 2 feet
HARDINESS: 10 to 11, annual elsewhere
USE: Screen, Vertical accent

Do a bit of research before planting. Morning glories are invasive in some regions and should not be planted. Others can use this twining vine on fences and trellises for a seasonal screen, vertical accent and the white, blue or purple flowers. Avoid excess water and fertilizer that can discourage flowering.

Passion Vine
Passiflora
MATURE HEIGHT X SPREAD: 5 to 20 feet x 1 to 3 feet
HARDINESS: 6 to 10
USE: Screen, Vertical accent

Take a close look at the purple, white or red summer flower and you will want to make room for this lovely vine. Edible fruit develops in areas where the season is warm and long. Northern gardeners may want to grow this in a container and overwinter it indoors.

design it yourself

This section contains a few tools to help you with your landscape plan. The focus is on using space and color to your best advantage. It's important to know the size of the space you'll be working with, and how to make the best use of color for maximum impact. You can plan to incorporate furniture and other non-plant elements to create your own retreat.

What You'll Find

- **Use the templates on page 166** to help you draw a plan for placing furniture, plants, and containers in your own small space garden. Consider whether you have space for items such as tables and chairs among your desired plants and trees.
- **Use the color wheel on page 167** to help you get a sense of color combinations that work. As described in chapter 2, the wheel will help with mixing and matching colors in the garden. Colors across from each other on the wheel are considered complementary, creating contrast and a focal point when placed next to each. Related colors, those next to each other on the wheel, blend and flow together.

You can color the template shapes you use to give you a feel of how flower and furniture colors will look together. Consider coloring the elements different colors based on the changing plant colors throughout the season. For example a small flowering tree such as amelanchier, will have white flowers in spring, green leaves in summer and brilliant red fall color.

Some gardeners use old catalogues and cut out pictures of the plants they plant to include. You could cut them to the size of the appropriate template (see size scale). This will give you a better sense of the color and texture of the plants you will be including.

Now share your plan with others who will use the space or friends with a good eye for space and design. Once you make sure the space works for everyone's needs you are ready to finalize the plan, purchase the plants and start creating your garden retreat.

Colors, such as the violets, silvers, and blues of this combination of plectranthus, juniper, and angelonia, have a calming effect and tend to appear further away than they are.

design diagrams

Find or purchase a piece of plain or graph paper. Draw the outline of your small space, as described in chapter 1, so that a $^1/_4$-inch square equals 1 square foot of space. Trace the templates that apply to your furniture and plant selections. Cut them out and try placing them in different areas around the space. Try several arrangements of plants, furnishings and accessories. Allow space for people to mingle and move through the area. Remember, when it comes to small spaces, less is usually better.

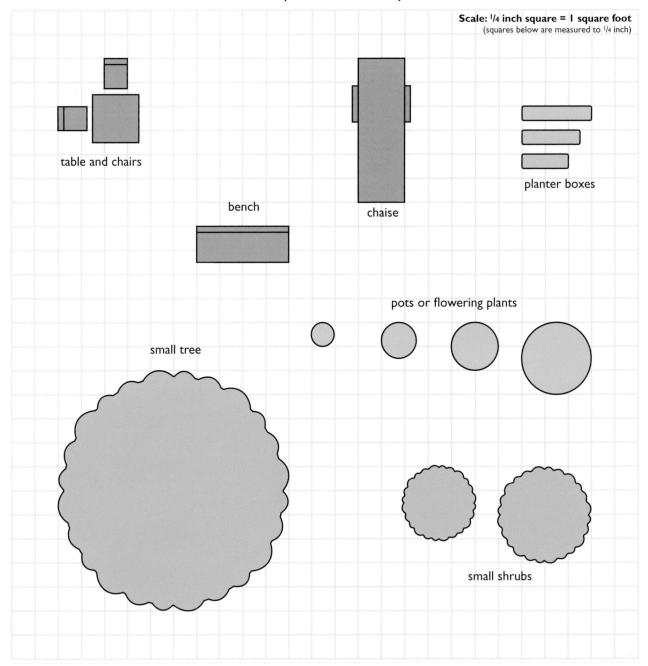

Scale: $^1/_4$ inch square = 1 square foot
(squares below are measured to $^1/_4$ inch)

table and chairs

bench

chaise

planter boxes

pots or flowering plants

small tree

small shrubs

color wheel

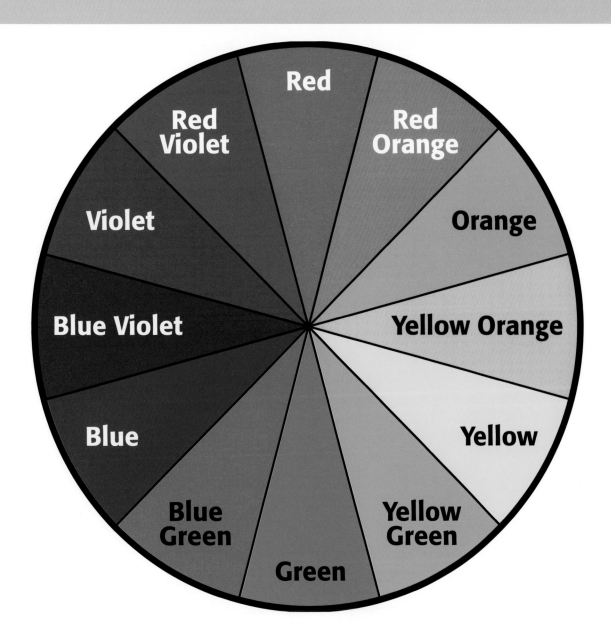

Cut a triangle out of paper, making it large enough so that when placed on top of the color wheel, one corner touches the yellow bar, one touches the red bar, and the 3rd corner touches the blue bar. **Tip:** *This combination of the three primary colors is always a winner.* When you turn the triangle around in the center of the color wheel each corner points to a different color. Colors in these combinations of 3's give you even more color combinations to use in your garden.

   Keep seasonal changes in mind when selecting all your plants and furnishings. Good news: nature has a way of making every color combination work on some level. And if something doesn't work, you can always make needed adjustments next season.

usda cold hardiness zones

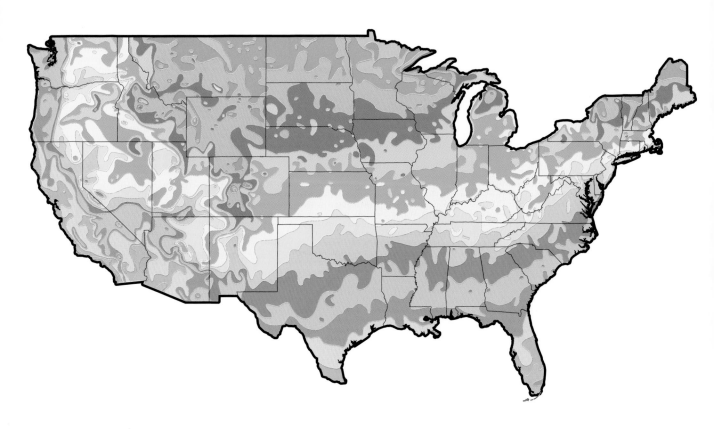

ZONE	Average Annual Minimum Temperature (°F)	ZONE	Average Annual Minimum Temperature (°F)	ZONE	Average Annual Minimum Temperature (°F)
2B	-40 to -45	5B	-10 to -15	8B	20 to 15
3A	-35 to -40	6A	-5 to -10	9A	25 to 20
3B	-30 to -35	6B	0 to -5	9B	30 to 25
4A	-25 to -30	7A	5 to 0	10A	35 to 30
4B	-20 to -25	7B	10 to 5	10B	40 to 35
5A	-15 to -20	8A	15 to 10	11	40 and Above

plant index